S0-ARO-121

GROUNDWORK GUIDES

Series Editor
Jane Springer

AUG 20 2009

Holliston Public Library
Holliston, MA 01746

GROUNDWORK GUIDES

Democracy
James Laxer

Groundwood Books
House of Anansi Press

Toronto Berkeley

Holliston Public Library
Holliston, MA 01746   AUG 20 2009

Copyright © 2009 by James Laxer
Published in Canada and the USA in 2009 by Groundwood Books

All rights reserved. No part of this publication may be reproduced, stored in a retrieval system or transmitted, in any form or by any means, without the prior written consent of the publisher or a license from The Canadian Copyright Licensing Agency (Access Copyright). For an Access Copyright license, visit www.accesscopyright.ca or call toll free to 1-800-893-5777.

Groundwood Books / House of Anansi Press
110 Spadina Avenue, Suite 801, Toronto, Ontario M5V 2K4
or c/o Publishers Group West
1700 Fourth Street, Berkeley, CA 94710

We acknowledge for their financial support of our publishing program the Canada Council for the Arts, the Government of Canada through the Book Publishing Industry Development Program (BPIDP) and the Ontario Arts Council.

ONTARIO ARTS COUNCIL
CONSEIL DES ARTS DE L'ONTARIO

Library and Archives Canada Cataloguing in Publication
Laxer, James
Democracy / James Laxer.
(A Groundwork guide)
Includes index.
ISBN 978-0-88899-912-2 (bound).–ISBN 978-0-88899-913-9 (pbk.)
1. Democracy. 2. Globalization. 3. Economic policy.
4. Sustainable development. I. Title. II. Series: Groundwork guides
JC423.L39 2009   321.8   C2008-905685-X

Design by Michael Solomon
Printed and bound in Canada

Contents

To Michael, Kate, Emily and Jonathan

Chapter 1
What Is Democracy?

In the West, citizens assume that they live in a democracy. By this they mean that they have the right to vote in elections to choose the people who will hold positions of power in the various levels of government in their country. They feel that they can express themselves freely on the issues of the day, holding whatever opinions they wish on the political leadership of their country without fearing negative reprisals for disagreeing with those in power.

When they think about democracy, it is natural for people to contrast it with dictatorship — a system of government in which one party or political leadership holds power, there are no fair elections among various political parties, and expressing negative views about the party in power or the leaders of the country could lead to a knock on the door from the police, to imprisonment, and in extreme cases to assassination or execution.

The word "democracy" is derived from the Greek and it means rule by the people. The ancient Greeks who developed the concept of democracy had no problem with the existence of slavery within a democracy — with the idea that citizens should have full rights while slaves could be treated like beasts of burden. In the city-state of Athens in the fifth century BC, for instance, citizens were expected to participate in the affairs of government and to take a direct role in the decision-making process. Only adult males over eighteen years of age had the right to participate. Slaves and women, as well as non-citizens who had a right to live in Athens, were barred from such participation. Involvement in Athenian democracy, therefore, extended only to a minority of the population, perhaps 20 percent of adults.

Democracy in modern nation-states almost always takes the form of "representative" democracy. That is to say, the citizens elect officeholders at various levels of government (municipal, state or provincial, federal or national), and those elected serve as the representatives of the people.

In ancient Athens, the system was one of "direct" democracy. Under such a system, all of the citizens gathered in a forum a number of times a year to make decisions. In Athens, the Assembly, attended by all citizens who were in the city and able to be present, met ten times a year and held additional meetings when necessary. The Assembly made major decisions regarding the granting of citizenship, the election of certain officials, and whether to go to war or to pass pieces of legislation. Speakers argued the case for and against particular propositions, and then the Assembly decided in a show-of-hands vote. Thousands of citizens took part in these meetings, and for certain types of decisions a quorum of six thousand citizens had to be in attendance.

Another key governing body in Athens was the Council of Five Hundred. The members of this body were selected by lottery each year from among the citizens who were thirty years of age or older. Citizens were allowed to serve on the Council twice in their lives. The Council prepared draft legislation for the Assembly, and in some instances it put the Assembly's legislation into effect.

The courts were also crucial to the Athenian system, and their jury panels were selected by lot from among citizens at least thirty years of age. Depending on the type of case involved, whether it was a public action brought against someone or a private suit, the number of jurors varied. There were no judges.

To the Athenian citizens of those times, the system of democracy that exists in nation-states today would seem highly undemocratic. They would be deeply suspicious of a system in which millions of citizens living in a large territory elect professional politicians from competing political parties to represent them. How can you trust such politicians? they would lament. And how can you entrust them with so much power for such long periods of time? To the practitioners of direct democracy (a system that could work in theory in a small city-state today, with all citizens having the right to participate), representative democracy appears to permit the citizen to do little more than vote every few years, while leaving the actual passing of legislation up to the professionals.

These criticisms have been voiced by many analysts in our own time and over the past two and a quarter centuries during which the modern democracies have developed. Jean Jacques Rousseau, writing in the eighteenth century, believed that a city the size of his native Geneva had the ideal population for a democracy.[1] In such a setting, direct democracy, the kind he favored, could flourish.

In our own era, the participants in the anti-globalization movements that have sprung up in many countries over the past two decades regard the decision-making process in contemporary nation-states as highly bureaucratic and undemocratic. They believe that the major states have fallen under the effective rule of multinational corporations that pursue strategies resulting in the exploitation and impoverishment of much of the world. To these often young activists who appear at summits of the leaders of the top industrial nations (the G8) or meetings of the International Monetary Fund or the World Bank, a new world order is needed to eliminate poverty and exploitation, and a system of real democracy is required. Usually, the anti-globalization activists have in mind a much more localized, decentralized economic system that in addition to representative government would allow workers to have control over their workplaces.

Essential features of contemporary democracy are the rights to free speech and assembly. Democracy also extends to the rule of law, to the right of those accused of crimes to fair and speedy trials, to freedom from arbitrary detention and to the right to legal counsel. As an essen-

Democracy in the Workplace

In a democracy, it is taken for granted that men and women have the right to participate in the political process and to vote in free and fair elections to select those who will govern them. The large majority of adults, however, spend only a very small portion of their lives engaging in politics. Where they do spend an enormous part of their active lives is in the workplace. Do the principles that underlie democracy apply in the workplace, and if not, should they? This conundrum has confounded theorists, politicians and trade unionists for the past two centuries.

In developed countries, wage and salary earners (who constitute about 70 percent of the total labor force) work in the office, factory, hospital or construction site, where they follow the instructions of their superiors. There, free speech is at a minimum. An employee who is heard by his or her manager saying things critical of the enterprise or the management is likely to be fired or at least issued with a serious warning.

Over the decades, there have been proposals for what has been called "workers' participation" or "workers' control" in decision-making within enterprises. The principles underlying these notions are much the same as those that are the foundation of political democracy.

In truth, no society in human history, at least since primitive times, has enjoyed anything close to economic democracy, that is to say, a set of arrangements through which the majority of the population sets the goals of the economy and enjoys the lion's share of its output. There was nothing democratic about the economic arrangements of ancient or feudal societies. Despite the claims of its adherents that Soviet Communism would evolve into a society that was fully democratic economically as well as politically, the Soviet Union was in its worst days a totalitarian state and in its latter days an authoritarian state in which neither political nor economic democracy was achieved.

What about economic democracy in today's advanced capitalist countries? A fundamental barrier in the way of economic democracy is the decision-making process that is inherent in an economy in which the private sector is dominant. In a democratic political system, men and women cast votes and are in that sense equal. In the economic system, it is not individual citizens who vote, it is dollars, euros or yen. In a company that is not publicly traded, ownership and control are in the hands of those who own the capital that sustains the activities of the enterprise. The owners hire the managers and are free to terminate their employment at will. The managers hire wage and salary earners, direct their activities in the workplace and can terminate their employment subject to the regulations discussed above.

In a publicly traded private-sector enterprise, control of the company is in the hands of the investors who hold sufficient voting shares to install and control the firm's management. Such a firm, because it is publicly traded, is open to the prospect of being taken over by another enterprise through the purchase of its voting shares. Such takeovers are common occurrences and they can be either "friendly" or "hostile." A friendly takeover is one that has the support of the current management, while a hostile takeover is the consequence of a power struggle against the wishes of the current management. Takeovers and mergers, where one firm merges with another to form a new corporate entity, are the consequence of votes being cast, but the votes are those of voting shares in the company, and they are denominated in the world's currencies and not in human beings.

Corporate consolidation has reached the point where

takeovers can involve many billions of dollars. For instance, in 2008, Microsoft attempted a hostile takeover of Yahoo for over $30 billion, while the managements of Yahoo and Google attempted to fend off the takeover.[2]

Is democracy compatible with an economic structure having top-down lines of authority and fundamental decisions based on control of capital and not on decisions made by those who work for a firm?

There have long been ideas about how to extend democracy into the economy. Over the past couple of centuries, utopian communities have been set up in many countries with the goal of pioneering the creation of a new kind of society with much different relationships among people. Most of the utopias collapse within a few years, leaving a bad taste in the mouths of those who tried the experiment. Some utopias last longer and can even claim to have some intellectual and artistic impact on the wider society. Utopias have been marginal affairs, however.

Over the past several decades, during the so-called age of globalization, ever larger pools of capital have been assembled under the control of ever more powerful financial institutions. The power of these entities that control and direct so many of the world's enterprises has become so vast that few nation-states can stand up to them. They have an enormous capacity to decide where investments will or will not go, and under what conditions. That fact puts the issue of the control of capital squarely on the democratic agenda and along with it the issue of democracy in the workplace.

tial aspect of rights in democratic states, there are guarantees that people will not face discrimination on the grounds of gender, race, religion, sexual orientation or age. While democracy encompasses the rights of majorities to do many important things, it does not encompass the right to discriminate against or to abuse minorities.

If democracy is about the right of the majority to elect the government of their choice while respecting the rights of minorities, what about the rights of individuals or groups to dissent from the policies of the government? While democrats would agree with the proposition that individuals should have the right to express their views and to assemble with others to put forward their ideas, what about the right to disobey the law to promote one's view of what is just? Is there a role for civil disobedience in a democratic society?

Democracy includes the rights of wage and salary earners to organize unions to represent them and to go on strike to bargain with their employers for higher salaries and better working conditions. It involves as well the rights of citizens, not only to elect governments and to run for office, but to petition those in power, to hold mass demonstrations to make their views known, and to organize themselves into the many bodies and institutions that comprise "civil society," which are neither a part of the state nor of the marketplace.

In the eyes of many social activists, trade unionists, civil rights advocates and political thinkers, the customary summary of what democracy entails is far too limited. Critics of the traditional view insist that true democracy involves much more than a set of formal institutions that permit people to elect their rulers — it includes the quest for economic and social justice. Without the achievement of greater social equality, they believe, democracy, even in the more limited sense, is imperiled today. This is the case not only in the developing world, where millions of people are forced to work for survival wages, but in the developed world too. In the wealthy countries, a large percentage of the population — disproportionately made up of indigenous people, immigrants, racial minorities, women and children — lives below the poverty line. In addition, full educational opportunity is not available to these people.

There are tangible reasons why democracy is in peril today in the wealthy countries. Over the past several decades, the gulf between the rich and the rest of the population has yawned ever wider, both in terms of income and wealth. During the same period, as a consequence of privatization of state-owned companies and the deregulation of economic activity, the role of the state and through it the role of the electorate has been appreciably reduced in favor of decisions made by giant firms on the basis of dollars, yen and euros rather than the votes of citizens.

Vast economic inequality is a potent foe of democracy. In the rich countries, this threat is growing ever greater.

Chapter 2
The Historical Rise of Democracy

Democracy has origins in diverse societies, including those of the ancient Greeks and Romans, but it evolved in modern times in the struggles for social equality and liberty during the seventeenth to nineteenth centuries in Europe and North America. These struggles, buttressed by new concepts of human nature as well as by revolutionary breakthroughs in science and philosophy, culminated in a massive assault on the established order. The American and French Revolutions in the latter decades of the eighteenth century were climactic episodes in that struggle.

Democracy rose along with capitalism. In Europe, the transition from feudalism to capitalism took centuries. Cities burgeoned and commerce flourished. Merchants and other wealthy city dwellers challenged the political authority of the aristocrats, wanting a place in the system of state power for themselves. Feudal society had rested on two major social classes, aristocratic landowners and the serfs who labored on their estates. In the cities, merchants and those they employed, as well as craftsmen —

jewelers, clockmakers, carpenters, gunsmiths, locksmiths, coopers, toolmakers and tailors — and their apprentices were actors in the creation of a new economy.

In France, the most populous country in western Europe, the system of government was out of step with the economic and social realities of the times. At the center of the state was the monarchy. Louis XIV, who reigned from 1643, when he was only five years old (he assumed personal control of the government in 1661), to his death in 1715, centralized the affairs of state around his court. The symbol of his growing power was the luxurious royal palace he had built at Versailles just outside Paris. In this sumptuous setting, one of the great architectural achievements of the age, the Sun King (as Louis XIV was known) ran the affairs of state, with the most powerful nobles gathered around him seeking his favor and influence. Shifting the capital to Versailles from Paris was a disdainful denial of the realities of capitalist France, which continued to develop out of sight of the royal court.

Beneath the monarchy, French society was divided into three categories called estates. The First Estate was composed of the Roman Catholic clergy, all the way from cardinals, archbishops and bishops to parish priests, monks and nuns. The nobility, those with aristocratic titles, were the members of the Second Estate. There were two types of nobles — the Nobles of the Sword, mostly great landowners and military men who had inherited their titles, and the Nobles of the Robe, rising lawyers and great merchants from the cities who received their titles from the king. Finally, there was the Third Estate — the rest of the population. The Third Estate comprised the vast majority of the French people, including merchants, bankers, craftsmen, common laborers and the serfs who toiled on the land.

As France fought great wars against its competitors for mastery in Europe as well as wars against Britain for a share of power in the wider world (especially in North America), the costs of the French state soared. Over the course of the eighteenth century, the state was desperate for new sources of revenue. In 1789, the threat of state bankruptcy forced the king's ministers to reach out to the members of the three estates to keep the treasury afloat. The need for revenue brought on the crisis that led to the French Revolution and the demise of the French state system.

The chronic difficulties of the state were not the only realities pressing France and Europe toward a new social order. Along with the new technologies of the period — most importantly the printing press and gunpowder — the established order of society was under relentless attack from the new perceptions of scientists and the writings of philosophers, satirists and other critics. The scientists, in particular Galileo, Copernicus and Newton, tore away at the assumed order of things. Instead of an order in which God, the Creator, had made the earth, placing it at the center, around which the sun, the moon and the stars revolved, they perceived a universe in which the earth revolved around the sun, and matter moved according to a set of natural laws that could be discovered and understood.

In this natural world, thinkers challenged the assumption that kings were divinely appointed and that aristocrats were naturally superior to common people. In England, seventeenth-century philosophers Thomas Hobbes and John Locke wrote of a world in which, in essential respects, all men (not women) were equal; all were mortal and doomed to perish. In such a world, Locke concluded that there needed to be a contract or understanding between those who governed and the people they governed. This idea was to have an enormous effect on the course of political thinking and the development of democracy in the American colonies and later, in the United States.

In France, the writings of Rousseau and Voltaire and other philosophers ridiculed and satirized the pretensions of those who held power. As France headed toward its own revolution, the first great revolution of modern times took place on the other side of the Atlantic. On July 4, 1776, the delegates to the Continental Congress, representing the thirteen British colonies, proclaimed their independence from Britain and established the United States of America. The Declaration of Independence went far beyond a claim that the colonists had the right to govern themselves. It asserted that "all men are created equal," and that they have the right to "life, liberty and the pursuit of happiness."[1]

By the time the Declaration was adopted the political collision between the colonists and the mother country had been underway for years. The colonists objected to taxes imposed on them by the distant government in

London and protested at the idea that Britain could maintain a standing army in America. At first the colonists claimed that they were fighting for the rights of Englishmen, but as time passed the struggle became national in character. Colonists were becoming Americans. Increasingly, they were fighting for the right to rule themselves. On April 19, 1775, at the Old North Bridge outside Concord, Massachusetts, British soldiers and colonial militias came to blows. It was there that the famed "shot heard round the world" was fired.[2] The Revolutionary War raged until 1783, when the British government agreed in the Treaty of Paris negotiated with representatives of the United States to recognize the independence of the new country.

Although the United States adopted a first constitution in 1781, it was in Philadelphia in 1787 that the delegates of the states met to draft the Constitution that has endured to this day. General George Washington, who had commanded the patriot armies against the British military during the Revolutionary War, was chosen to chair the constitutional convention. The Constitution was drafted and adopted, one by one, by the thirteen American states, thereby coming into force. The democratic character of the Constitution is revealed in its first three words: "We the people…" The idea that "the people" through their chosen representatives should draft their own Constitution and establish their own form of government challenged the way virtually every other country in the world was governed at the time.

The Constitution established the institutions of representative government in the United States. There was to be a president, who was to be chief executive and commander in chief of the armed forces. Two Houses of Congress, a House of Representatives, with a two-year term, and a Senate, with a six-year term, were created. The powers of the federal government and the state governments were enumerated. A Supreme Court was established, having the job of determining whether legislation passed by the Congress or by the states fell within their respective jurisdictions, and whether such legislation adhered to the terms of the Constitution. A formula for amending the Constitution was included.

In 1789, a series of amendments was proposed and ten of these came into force in 1791. These first ten amendments to the Constitution are known as the Bill of Rights. They spell out the rights of citizens and they limit the power of the government. The Congress is not allowed to pass laws that violate the propositions set out in these additions to the Constitution. The First Amendment, one of the most fundamental, reads as follows: "Congress shall make no law respecting an establishment of religion, or prohibiting the free exercise thereof; or abridging the freedom of speech, or of the press; or the right of the people peaceably to assemble, and to petition the Government for a redress of grievances."

Other amendments guaranteed the right of citizens not to incriminate themselves, the right to a jury trial and protection from unreasonable search and seizure. They also prohibited the state from imposing excessive bail for those on trial and barred the state from inflicting cruel and unusual punishments on those found guilty of crimes. The Second Amendment, controversial as to how it should be interpreted, guaranteed the right to bear arms.

While the Constitution was much more democratic than the governing arrangements in other countries at the time, it also revealed the determination of its drafters not to allow democracy to operate unchecked. The president and vice-president, for instance, were not to be elected directly by the people. Instead, the drafters created a body called the Electoral College. In each state, the voters were to elect a slate of electors. Following the election, the electors from each state were to gather and to cast their ballots. The idea was to allow an elite group, rather than the people themselves, to pick the country's top officeholders. This system is still in place today. It plays little role, however, in the selection of the president and vice-president, since the major political parties, the Democrats and the Republicans, choose slates of electors in each state who will vote for their presidential candidate. Technically, it is these slates of electors for whom citizens cast their ballots, not the candidates themselves.

The drafters showed the same reluctance about democracy when it came to the Houses of Congress. While the House of Representatives was to be elected by the voters every two years and was to be based on representation by population (the representation of states was proportional to the size of their populations), the Senate was a different matter entirely. Senators, two for each state regardless of population, were to be selected for six years and were to be chosen by state legislators, not by the electorate.[3] This system remained in place until 1913, when an amendment to the Constitution stipulated that voters henceforth would directly elect their senators.

In 1789, matters came to a head in France. The revenue-starved government of Louis XVI decided to put the state's financial house in order and called a meeting of the Estates General. Once assembled in Paris, the leaders of the Third Estate demanded special powers for themselves, insisting that they represented the huge majority of the people of France. In the increasingly tense political atmosphere, they went on to declare that "the Third Estate is the nation," a fateful step that negated the legitimacy of the other two estates.

Next came the popular uprising in Paris that transformed the nation. On July 14, 1789, the forces of the revolution stormed the Bastille, a prison in Paris that symbolized the power of the old regime. A few weeks later, on August 4, 1789, the French National Constituent Assembly, which had become the voice of the Third Estate, abolished the rights of the nobility in France and transferred the great estates of the aristocrats to the serfs who worked the land. At one stroke what remained of feudalism was abolished; the serfs became farmers, owning their farms — a giant step toward the creation of a new society.

Three weeks after the abolition of feudal land tenure, the Assembly adopted the Declaration of the Rights of

Man and Citizen. The Declaration proclaimed the fundamental equality of all men (not women) and enumerated their fundamental rights. The most sweeping statement of rights adopted by any national government up until that time, the Declaration is a forerunner of the Universal Declaration of Human Rights passed by the United Nations in 1948. The first article of the Declaration reads: "Men are born free and equal in rights. Social distinctions may be founded only upon the general good." The second article states: "The aim of all political association is the preservation of the natural and imprescriptible rights of man. These rights are liberty, property, security, and resistance to oppression." (Imprescriptible means that the rights cannot be taken away.)

Over the next few years, political factions struggled for advantage in the National Assembly. The monarchy was abolished in 1792 and a republic was proclaimed in its place. The deposed Louis XVI and his wife, Marie Antoinette, fled but were captured and brought back to Paris, where they were ultimately executed by guillotine in 1793.[4]

From its initial steps toward democracy, France descended into the so-called Reign of Terror. Thousands of former aristocrats, as well as political opponents of those in power, were put to death. A new and more conservative regime known as the Directory assumed power in 1795. Not long after, General Napoleon Bonaparte, who had successfully led French armies against foreign foes, emerged as a strongman. In 1804, he assumed the

First-Past-the-Post Versus Proportional Representation

In the democratic world, there are two broadly different systems for electing governments, "first-past-the-post" and "proportional representation" or "PR." The first-past-the-post system is used today in the United States, the United Kingdom and Canada for the election of representatives at all levels of government (except for the election of members of the European Parliament in the UK, in which a version of proportional representation is in place).

First-past-the-post is easy to understand. In each constituency, district or ward, the candidate who places first after one round of voting wins and does not require a majority of the votes cast for victory. The system has its roots in a time before there were clearly established political parties.

In the British parliamentary system in place in the UK and Canada, to form a government a political party needs (by itself or in alliance with another party or parties) to have the support of a majority of members of the House of Commons. There need not be a formal coalition in a case where the leading party has fewer than 50 percent of the seats. The government stays in power for up to five years unless a majority of the members of the House of Commons votes nonconfidence in it, causing the government to fall, which normally triggers a general election.

The strength and weakness of first-past-the-post (depending on your point of view) is that even when there are more than two significant parties contesting an election, one party often emerges with a majority of seats and forms what is called a majority government. The advantage is that even if the winning party gained only about 40 percent of the vote, it can win a substantial majority of seats and form a stable government that can govern for four or five years. The disadvantage is that as many as 60 percent of voters (even more in rare cases) have cast their ballots for parties other than the one that holds power.

In a case where the ideas and platform of the winning party are passionately opposed by the majority of voters, the first-past-the-post system can alienate much of the population from the utility of the political system. This happened in Britain beginning in 1979 when Margaret Thatcher's Conservatives won the first of three consecutive majority governments while never winning more than 44 percent of the popular vote. The Thatcher government transformed Britain's society and economy, despite the opposition of the majority of voters to its program.

Similarly in Canada, during the general election in 1988, Canadian society was deeply polarized over whether the country should opt for the Free Trade Agreement with the US that had been negotiated by the Progressive Conservative government of Prime Minister Brian Mulroney. The election became a virtual national referendum on the free trade issue. The Conservatives campaigned for the agreement, while the Liberals and the New Democratic Party, the two major opposition parties, campaigned against it. On election day, the Conservatives won 43 percent of the popular vote, and the Liberals and the NDP, between them, won the support of 53 percent of voters. The resulting Conservative government ratified the Free Trade Agreement, which came into effect a few weeks later, despite the fact that the majority of voters had opted for parties committed to rejecting the trade deal.

Although the US does not have a parliamentary system of government, elections of members of the House of Representatives and the Senate are first-past-the-post affairs, and so too is the election of the president, state by state and through the arcane method of electing members of the Electoral College who formally choose the president.

There are many variations on the basic theme of proportional representation, although they all are based on a single premise – that votes cast for parties other than the leading party should also count in choosing representatives and in shaping the makeup of governments.

The idea is that parties should be represented in a legislative chamber in proportion to the number of votes they receive, thus eliminating the electoral distortions that plague first-past-the-post.

A good example of proportional representation is the one used in the Federal Republic of Germany since the creation of the republic in 1949. The German system is called "personalized proportional representation," and it is used in the election of members of the Bundestag, the lower house in the German parliament. With this system, each voter casts two votes, one for a member of the electoral district in which he or she lives and one for the voter's preferred political party.

The member elected for the local constituency is selected in a first-past-the-post contest – the candidate with the most votes wins. Then the second vote comes into play, the vote for a political party. It is used to achieve a fair balance among the parties by compensating for the distortions left following the vote for members to represent constituencies. Let's say that the party receiving 42 percent of the votes won 65 percent of the constituency races, while the party coming second won 38 percent of the votes and 35 percent of the constituency contests. Meanwhile three other parties, between them, received 20 percent of the vote and won none of the constituency races.

What then happens is that in addition to the victors in the constituency races, the parties that were under-represented in the distribution of seats are granted extra seats in the Bundestag. In our example, here is the outcome. The first party, having won a higher proportion of constituency races than its percentage of the popular vote, wins no extra seats. The second party is awarded extra seats to bring its 35 percent of constituencies won up to a 38 percent share of representation in the Bundestag – the latter percentage, the proportion of votes it won. Meanwhile the three smaller parties that between them received 20 percent of the votes, while winning no constituencies, receive seats in the Bundestag up to 20 percent of the total.

The extra seats go to candidates on lists drawn up by each political party and published in advance of the election. The candidates on the lists are numbered by the parties, beginning with their first choice, then their second and so on. The members added to the Bundestag from party lists have the same status in parliament as the members elected in constituencies.

Under the German system, only political parties that gain at least 5 percent of the popular vote receive seats in the Bundestag derived from the party lists. The founders of the Federal Republic were determined to avoid a situation in which ever more political parties are created and awarded seats. This could result in the splintering of representation, opening the door to small and unrepresentative political parties gaining leverage over governments by offering them support to keep them in office in exchange for political concessions. (Such splintering has been the outcome in a number of states, including Weimar Germany during the 1920s and early 1930s and Israel and Italy in recent decades.)

Germany's voting system has played an important role in providing six decades of stable governments reflecting a wide range of significant political views. Four of the five political parties that currently have seats in the Bundestag have been included in the coalitions that have governed the country.

Critics of proportional representation argue that unlike first-past-the-post, PR seldom results in the election of a majority government in which one party can rule on its own. It's true that German elections almost never result in a majority of seats in the Bundestag being won by a single party. But is this really a negative feature? A consequence of the German electoral system has been to stamp a centrist character on German governments. No single party's ideas can wholly shape the policies of a government, and effective political leaders need to hone conciliatory as well as combative political skills.

office of Emperor of the French following a plebiscite, a vote of the French electorate that approved this step.

Despite what followed it, the revolution changed the basic structure of society, ending feudal privileges and opening the way for a modern capitalist society in which, in theory at least, all men (but again, not women) were equal. The ideas of the revolution, in part as a result of the occupation of much of Europe by Napoleon's armies, spread far beyond the borders of France.

The principles, and to some extent the practice, of democracy and human rights had become fundamental notions of Western civilization. Despite huge setbacks, dictatorial regimes and authoritarian monarchies in many European countries, these ideas and aspirations became a permanent part of the societal landscape.

With the victory of capitalism over the remnants of feudalism and aristocratic rule, however, some thinkers and activists challenged what they saw as the limits of capitalist democracy. For these socialists, and later social democrats, capitalist democracy privileged the domination of society by those who owned land and controlled capital at the expense of wage and salary earners. To liberalism's insistence on equality of opportunity, these advocates advanced the case that full democracy needed to include equality of condition, by which they meant a much fuller share of material and cultural benefits of society for the whole of the population.

Historically, democracy emerged — but not because of a general tendency for human life to improve over time and to become more progressive. Democracy did not

Democracy and Economic Growth

Totalitarian and authoritarian states can also be the setting for a rapidly growing economy and rising living standards. Nazi Germany experienced strong economic growth during the 1930s, and living standards rose under the Hitler regime even during the first two years of the Second World War. In China today, with its one-party system of government and the regime's brutal repression of demands for free speech, human rights and political pluralism, there has been enormous economic growth and rapidly rising living standards for a large minority of the population with no corresponding trend toward democracy. In the West, the case has often been made that as China prospers, is drawn into the global trading system and becomes the site for ever larger amounts of foreign investment, the country will evolve toward the rule of law and the establishment of human rights and political democracy. Yet so far, there is little concrete evidence that China's economic engagement with the rest of the world has opened the way toward democracy.

develop because of some basic law of nature that as human beings become more adept technologically and living standards rise, human rights and political rights are bound to follow. Democracy developed in a particular historical setting as a consequence of a vast struggle for power in an economic and social order that was undergoing an enormous transformation. On the western rim of Europe, as towns and cities rose, based on the commerce of merchants, craftsmen and bankers, a new capitalist society found itself in conflict with the established social and political structure in which an aristocratic landowning class reaped the fruits of peasant labor.

The wealthy bourgeoisie that rode the wave of this great change found itself confined and constricted in the existing arrangements for the exercise of power. For it to achieve the place in the sun to which wealth and ambition seemed to entitle its members, revolution was necessary. In Britain, the revolution progressed from the seventeenth to the nineteenth centuries without a complete overturning of the old order. In France, it took place in a much shorter period.

To achieve victory, the bourgeoisie and its political and intellectual allies had to array the broad mass of the population, including the peasantry and urban laborers, as well as the organized power of women (in protests to reduce the price of bread, for instance) on its side. (This was not the first time in history that members of the upper classes made use of the weight of the lower classes to realize their own societal ends. In Rome, in the first century BC, upper-class contenders for power, among them Julius Caesar, mobilized the Roman masses through "bread and circuses" to defeat their opponents.)

Philosophically, the concept that underlay the right of all men (and later women) to a say in choosing those who would govern them was the idea that in fundamental respects all people are equal. Equality as a concept rested on the hopeful idea that people were essentially rational and capable, through education, of becoming ever more rational. In our day, the broad case for human rights and democracy rests on these same constructs, despite the fact that contemporary theories of psychology are far less optimistic about human rationality. Democracy, as we know it, has been just as much an invention as any other human construct. It does not arise in some inevitable way out of human nature.

The Continuing Evolution of Democracy

Having achieved victory by summoning the power of the mass of the population, the political representatives of the bourgeoisie soon showed themselves to be anxious to limit the power of the people. The 1787 US Constitution was decidedly less democratic than were the expressions of the earlier phases of the American Revolution. In France, the revolution shifted decisively in a conservative direction after 1794 with the rise of Napoleon Bonaparte to the position of emperor.

Democracy though, has proved to be a hardy construct. Once set in motion, it is not so easy to halt or to reverse, although this certainly has occurred in various societies over the past two centuries. Through the American and French Revolutions, the aspirations of farmers and laborers, women and racial minorities, and not just those of merchants, bankers and the new industrialists, had been whetted.

In the United States, populist movements in the 1820s and 1830s (e.g., Jacksonian Democrats named after Andrew Jackson, president of the United States from 1829 to 1837), fueled by the westward migration of the population and the occupation of new farmland, successfully grappled with the financial interests of the East.

In France, in 1830, again in 1848 and in the enormous upheaval of the Paris Commune in 1871, revolutionary outbursts brought the demands of working people to the fore. Democracy was not left to the bourgeoisie that had triumphed in the eighteenth-century revolutions.

In the US, the Civil War struggle from 1861 to 1865, which ended with the abolition of slavery, was succeeded in the 1890s and the first decade of the twentieth century by the movement of progressives who gave voice to the discontent of farmers oppressed by the power of banks. Throughout the same decades, workers' movements erupted in fury against low wages and miserable working conditions. Strikes were violently suppressed. During World War I, Eugene Debs, the jailed socialist candidate for president, managed to win a million votes.

In Europe, as well, battles for the rights of working people, waged by socialists and anarchists of many stripes, broke out and were in turn followed by waves of repression. On both continents, democratic struggles during these decades also focused on the issue of the right of women to vote. The suffragettes (women fighting for the right of women to vote) in Europe and North America were met with furious resistance, but they ultimately prevailed. The working-class movements during the Great Depression of the 1930s fused eventually with the much wider political alliance that underlay the military coalition against Nazism, fascism and Japanese militarism in the Second World War.

In the West, the postwar decades opened the way to a democracy that was social as well as political. In Canada and in Europe, democratic achievements included rising incomes for workers, greater job security, vastly improved social programs and wider access to higher education. In the United States, in the 1950s and 1960s, the civil rights movement won its historic victories against segregation and for the political rights of African Americans.

In the 1960s, a cultural war with important societal implications pitted an enormous part of the younger generation against the established order in North America and in Europe. In 1968, matters came to a head in these democratic struggles. Following the assassinations of Martin Luther King and Robert Kennedy earlier that year, young people who were disillusioned with the political establishment took to the streets of Chicago in the thousands during the Democratic Party's National Convention. As the city police assaulted them, they chanted to the television cameras, "The whole world's watching." In Paris that year, a movement for change brought hundreds of thousands of students, youths and workers into the streets, culminating in a general strike of ten million people that threatened to topple the regime of President Charles de Gaulle.

The established order remained intact in the face of these challenges, but seeds were sown for the democratic struggles of the future.

The political core of the 1960s movements on both continents fractured into the futile politics of factionalism. New struggles, however — those of women and gays and lesbians — emerged in the 1970s, drawing on what had come before. The women's movement transformed the nature of politics. It became much more difficult for politicians to make rhetorical claims that they served the population without dealing in detail with the working lives of women and the realities of family existence. The gay and lesbian struggle achieved a profound deepening of the understanding of minority populations and shattered forever the conception that a single norm could comprehend the mainstream of human society.

Again, in the late 1990s, following a period of conservatism and political quiescence among the young, new movements arose to express opposition to the vastly unequal effects of globalization. This first large-scale upheaval of the young in the West in the post-Cold War period had its own distinctive political character. Disillusioned with political parties in the West and with Marxism in the aftermath of the collapse of the Soviet Union, the movement was self-consciously decentralist. It shunned the very idea of having established leaders, and to a much greater extent than during the 1960s and 1970s, women played vital roles both intellectually and politically.

The anti-globalization movement drew much of its political content and style from the anarchist theory and practice of the past century, with its emphasis on direct action. Anarchism has always had a problematic relationship with democracy. Anarchists have aspired to the elimination of the state, which they wish to replace with a cooperative social order. For them, the deed is the thing — the spectacular act of defiance that will both taunt the authorities to show their repressive character and demonstrate to the people the way to change society. The movement directed its energies to mounting huge protests against meetings of the International Monetary Fund (IMF), the World Bank and the G8 — for them the symbols of globalization.

In 1999, the movement came to the attention of the world with its enormous demonstrations and the mounting of a counter-summit in Seattle in opposition to a conclave of the World Trade Organization. In the spring of 2000, the movement targeted a meeting of the IMF and the World Bank in Washington, DC. In April 2001, demonstrators descended on Quebec City to protest a summit of the government leaders of the Western Hemisphere who were planning to launch the Free Trade Area of the Americas.

The terror attacks on New York and Washington on September 11, 2001, had a dramatic and negative impact on the anti-globalization movement. The attacks and their aftermath drove home the reality that the importance of the state had by no means diminished as a consequence of globalization. The outlook of the movement came to seem peripheral to the course of events. Moreover, the insistence of some anarchist groups on carrying out assaults on the police and on the physical sites where meetings were being held badly divided the movement. Anarchist violence, while previously dismissed by others as childish foolishness, seemed malevolent after September 11. The anti-globalization movement became a casualty of the terror attacks.

Democracy, history has shown, is constantly being

tested, reinvented, questioned, curtailed and in some cases eliminated altogether. A system of government in which the majority of the population has a crucial say is always prone to furtive or open attacks on its effectiveness from powerful interests who are determined to prevent popular assaults on their domination, or from religious or ideological movements that are fundamentally opposed to democracy, or crucial aspects of it, notably the rights of women.

Chapter 3
Democratic Rights for Women and Racial and Religious Minorities

The US Declaration of Independence and the French Declaration of the Rights of Man and Citizen proclaimed rights for men, but not for women. Women had to struggle for the right to vote, to hold public office and to enjoy the right to own and control property, free from the oversight of male relatives and husbands. They had to campaign for the right to attend institutions of higher learning and to practice professions alongside men. In some societies, those rights have not yet been secured.

The struggles for democratic rights for members of racial and religious minorities alert us to a crucial aspect of democracy — it is not all about the rights of majorities. If, for instance, the suppression of political rights for Jews, Muslims or non-Caucasians is supported by the majority of voters in a country, is it a true democracy? This is not a hypothetical question. Many regimes in history have denied political rights to minorities. In Britain, in the eighteenth century, for instance, Roman Catholics were not allowed to vote or to be elected to the House of Commons. In many countries, Jews were barred from voting. In Britain, for example, Jews were not accorded the full right to be elected to the House of Commons and then to be sworn in to take their seats until 1858.

Women's Political Rights

In both North America and Europe, the campaigns for political rights for women shared the common heritage and much of the language of the eighteenth-century struggles for the rights of man. Indeed, the British writer and feminist Mary Wollstonecraft published *A Vindication of the Rights of Woman* in 1792 in which she made the case that women are not naturally inferior to men, and that they too should be accorded full political rights.

Of necessity, individual struggles were waged within each country. While their aims were similar and campaigners drew sustenance from one another, tactics varied from country to country. What was common to all the campaigns was how difficult they were, how much resistance they faced and how long they took. To win the fight for the vote, women had to adopt militant tactics, engage in civil disobedience and spend time in jail.

In the United States, the arduous struggle of women to win the right to vote came with the passage of the Nineteenth Amendment of the US Constitution in August 1920. The amendment stated: "The right of citizens of the United States to vote shall not be denied or abridged by the United States or by any State on account of sex. Congress shall have power to enforce this article by appropriate legislation."

The battle that led to the Nineteenth Amendment was waged relentlessly over a period of seven decades. In 1848, in Seneca Falls, New York, pioneers in the fight for female suffrage, among them Elizabeth Cady Stanton and Lucretia Mott, gathered to plan their campaign. In the decades that followed the historic 1848 meeting, the struggle was waged both at the federal and state levels. For a long time the movement was divided over strategy, with two main organizations adopting different approaches.

The American Woman Suffrage Association, founded by Julia Ward Howe and Lucy Stone, included male as well as female members and combined the struggle for the right of women to vote with the campaign for black suffrage. The organization worked for the ratification of the Fifteenth Amendment to the US Constitution, which outlawed the denial of the right to vote on the grounds of race. (As we will see, the amendment did little to protect suffrage for blacks in the South.) Stanton and Mott, along with Susan B. Anthony, founded the alternative National Woman Suffrage Association for women only. The goal of their organization was a constitutional amendment to enshrine female suffrage in the United States. Prior to and during the Civil War, much of the energy that went into the early fight for female suffrage was diverted into the campaign against slavery.

In the late nineteenth and early twentieth centuries, energy from the female suffrage movement was channeled into the temperance struggle, the remarkable movement to ban the use of alcohol in the US. (Many feminists backed the temperance movement because of the huge losses of household income and upsurge in domestic violence associated with men's alcohol abuse.) A constitutional amendment banning the sale of alcohol in the United States came into effect in 1919 and was later repealed in 1933.

Victories in the fight for female suffrage came first at the state and local levels, and some of these victories pre-dated the concerted campaign that began in 1848. As early as 1776, women in New Jersey who had property worth $250 were allowed to vote but later lost that right. In 1837, some women in Kentucky were granted the right to vote in school board elections, and women in Kansas gained the same right in 1861 when that state was admitted to the Union. In 1869, in what was hailed as an important national victory, women in the Wyoming Territory won the right to vote and to hold public office. The following year, women in the Utah Territory won the vote. In a number of states, including Colorado, Washington, Michigan, Kansas, Oregon and Arizona, the male electorates voted to grant women the franchise in the years prior to the First World War. During the war itself, the campaign for women's votes reached its zenith, with some American women employing the more mili-tant tactics of their suffragette sisters in Britain who chained themselves to railings in front of public buildings and were arrested and hauled off to jail.[1]

In Canada, the path to women's suffrage was more tortuous. At the federal level, the first time women were allowed to vote was in the wartime election of 1917, and

Civil Disobedience

In 1846, New England writer Henry David Thoreau was jailed for one night for refusing to pay the poll tax in Massachusetts. The morning after Thoreau's night behind bars, he was released because, much to his displeasure, his aunt came forward to pay the tax on his behalf. In his essay, "Civil Disobedience," Thoreau explained the reasons for his refusal to pay the tax. The essay, regarded as a classic around the world, helped establish the rationale for the political movements of Mohandas Gandhi and Martin Luther King.

Thoreau's immediate objection to the poll tax was his disagreement with the war the US fought against Mexico between 1846 and 1848. He also associated the tax with slavery. But his broader objection cast into doubt the very legitimacy of the government and raised fundamental questions about the relationship between the individual and the state. Most important and controversial was Thoreau's insistence that a single individual has the right, indeed the duty, to resist the state, even a democratic state whose government is elected by the people, when he or she believes that the policies of the state are morally repugnant.

Thoreau's famous essay raised fundamental difficulties for democrats, and the issues it brought to the fore are debated as hotly today as they were then. Does a single person have the right to resist the will of a government that has been elected by a majority of the people and that is carrying out the will of the population? Is it not elitist, selfish, undemocratic and arrogant for an individual to claim that his or her moral objection should carry weight against the decisions of an elected government?

"The only obligation which I have a right to assume is to do at any time what I think right," wrote Thoreau, setting out his justification for disobeying the law.[2] His words have been repeated by peoples fighting for their rights ever since and have had an immense impact on political movements the world over.

"Thoreau was a great writer, philosopher, poet, and withal a most practical man, that is, he taught nothing he was not prepared to practice in himself," wrote Gandhi.[3] And in his biography, King acknowledged that Thoreau's was a "legacy of creative protest" and declared, "I became convinced that noncooperation with evil is as much a moral obligation as is cooperation with good."[4]

Even if it is nonviolent, as Gandhi and King insisted that it should be, civil disobedience will always have an uneasy relationship with democracy. Civil disobedience involves more than the right to protest, which is no more than an expression of the right to free speech about which no true democrat will raise an objection. It claims the right to challenge the laws of the country and the edicts of the government and to refuse to obey them. On the grounds of conscience, can such a philosophy be acceptable to democrats?

Here is a case in point. On December 1, 1955, Rosa Parks, a forty-two-year-old African American seamstress, was riding on a bus in Montgomery, Alabama. She refused to obey the "established rule" of the time that blacks had to sit at the back of the bus and when a white person wanted their seat, they had to surrender it. Mrs. Parks would not yield her seat to a white rider. She stayed peacefully in her place. The police were called and she was arrested.

Mrs. Parks had disobeyed the rules in a society in which the government was elected by the majority, although African American Alabamans were effectively excluded from the right to vote at the time. Her action inspired a social movement. Dr. Martin Luther King, who was pastor of the Dexter Avenue Baptist Church in the city, along with other African American community leaders, organized a protest to support her. Their weapon was a boycott. A few days after the arrest of Rosa Parks, African Americans refused to use the bus system in Montgomery until the rules consigning them to second-class status were removed. The organizers of the boycott provided bicycles, a few cars and in some cases animals to ride, and many walked. Since a large proportion of passengers on the bus system was African American, the boycott was highly effective and cut sharply into the bus company's revenues.

Vicious methods were used to try to break the boycott by the white establishment in Montgomery. Leaders were arrested, those waiting on the street for alternative methods of transport were sometimes arrested and charged with vagrancy, and the house of Martin Luther King was dynamited. Despite these pressures, the boycott held. After more than a year, the bus company relented and African Americans were allowed to ride on the buses on the same terms as white riders. Rosa Parks, who lived to be ninety-two, was celebrated as one of the great heroines of the civil rights movement for the rest of her days.

Civil disobedience continues to raise fundamental issues as well as to ignite blistering controversy. During the Vietnam War in the 1960s and 1970s, thousands of young men who had been drafted into the US armed forces left the country to seek asylum in Canada. The argument advanced by these men, as well by a smaller number of others who deserted from the US forces, was that the Vietnam War was an unjust conflict and that they were ethically compelled to refrain from engaging in it.

Canada allowed these draft resisters and deserters to remain on Canadian soil. While thousands of them returned to the US, taking advantage of the amnesty granted by the Clinton administration in 1994, thousands more took out Canadian citizenship and made a significant contribution to their new homeland in a host of fields.

Following the US invasion of Iraq in 2003, a small number of US servicemen deserted and made their way to Canada, again seeking refugee status. This time the Americans were turned down. In the summer of 2008, the Canadian immigration board and a Canadian court ruled that one of the first deserters to come to Canada had six weeks to leave the country.

they acquired the vote for highly partisan reasons. The issue in that election was whether Canada should conscript men to serve in the military so they could fight in the trenches in France. The Conservative government joined forces with the minority of Liberals who were pro-conscription and waged the campaign as the Unionists. Just before the election was called, the government altered the voting rules to allow women to vote, but only the women relatives of men who were in the armed forces. At the same time, the government revoked the right to vote from those who had been naturalized after March 1902 and were immigrants from Germany and Austria-Hungary, countries with which Canada was at war.

In 1918, parliament passed an act to allow all women to vote in federal elections. The act came into effect in 1919. In 1916, Manitoba, Saskatchewan and Alberta had amended their election acts to confer votes on women. The following year, British Columbia and Ontario took the same step, and over the next five years Nova Scotia, New Brunswick, the Yukon Territory and Prince Edward Island passed similar legislation. In Newfoundland (not yet a province of Canada), women over twenty-five years of age won the vote in 1925. Last among the provinces was Quebec, whose women did not obtain the vote in provincial elections until 1940. Finally, in the Northwest Territories, women did not receive the right to vote in territorial elections until 1951.

The achievement of female suffrage at the federal level in Canada by no means ended the legal inequality of

Canadian women. In 1927, one of the most famous legal cases in Canadian history was undertaken when five women — Emily Murphy, Henrietta Muir Edwards, Louise McKinney, Irene Parlby and Nellie McClung — launched the so-called *Persons* case, the goal being to win the right for women to be appointed to the Senate of Canada. In their petition, which went to the Supreme Court of Canada, the women sought clarification on whether the word "persons" in Section 24 of the British North America Act (Canada's constitution at the time), the section that dealt with Senate appointments, included female persons. The Supreme Court took on the case on March 14, 1928, and six weeks later issued its finding. Arguing that the BNA Act of 1867 needed to be interpreted according to the times in which it was written, the Court ruled that since women were not politically active at the time of Confederation they could not be appointed to the Senate. The women who had undertaken the legal challenge did not stop there but appealed the ruling to the Judicial Committee of the Privy Council in London (at that time the highest court of appeal for Canadian cases). In 1929, the members of the Judicial Committee ruled unanimously that "the word 'persons' in Section 24 includes both the male and female sex…." According to the high court, the exclusion of women from public office was "a relic of days more barbarous than ours."[5]

In Britain, the struggle for the franchise for women is remembered a century later as a great confrontation within British society. The movement was divided between the radical suffragettes and the more moderate suffragists. For both wings of the movement, the mid-nineteenth century writings of John Stuart Mill advocating votes for women were a common intellectual heritage. The British struggle took place against the backdrop of a wider democratic ferment that challenged the ethos of a society dominated politically, economically and culturally by an amalgam of aristocrats and financial capitalists.

The radical suffragettes engaged in civil disobedience to draw attention to their cause and to make it ever more difficult for the established order to function without having the issue of votes for women thrust at them. As well as chaining themselves to railings, members of the movement set fire to the contents of mailboxes and in some cases set off bombs. Women who were arrested sometimes resorted to hunger strikes and were force-fed in jail.

When the First World War broke out, the more moderate wing of the movement called a truce in its public campaign for votes for women, while the more militant wing continued its protests. The name Pankhurst is indelibly linked in the British mind with the struggle. Emmeline and Christabel Pankhurst were involved in the moderate Women's Social and Political Union, and Sylvia Pankhurst (daughter of Emmeline and sister of Christabel) led the Women's Suffrage Federation. The war transformed public attitudes to women, hundreds of thousands of whom entered the labor force to replace men who were fighting at the front. Thousands of others cared for and nursed wounded soldiers, both in France and England.

In 1918, the British parliament passed an act that extended the vote to women over the age of thirty who met certain financial qualifications or who were university graduates. In 1928, further legislation granted the vote to women on equal terms with men.[6]

Noteworthy for their early and effective struggles for female emancipation were the Scandinavian countries, in particular Norway. As Norwegian society industrialized and as local communities lost their position as the central locus of labor for both men and women, gender roles were transformed. As women entered the workforce, they formed feminist organizations to demand equal pay for their labor and to insist that women should have the right to vote. In 1884, the Norwegian Feminist Society was established, and a year later the fight for women's votes became the central concern of the newly created Female Suffrage Union. The twin struggles for equal pay and for the right to vote fractured Norwegian society, in some cases pitting men against women in the workplace. The women who took up the cause of female suffrage made the case that women would strengthen democracy in Norway, and that their voices would aid in the peaceful struggle to throw off the unwanted political union with Sweden. In 1905, Norway gained its national independence. Eight years later, on the eve of the First World War, all Norwegian women won the right to vote, putting them well ahead of their sisters in the US, Canada and the UK in achieving their goal.[7]

Women in New Zealand won the vote in 1893. Other leaders in granting female suffrage were Australia (1902) and Finland (1906). Toward the end of the First World War and immediately following the conflict, women gained the right to vote in the Soviet Union in 1917 (a right that soon became virtually meaningless for both women and men); Germany, Austria, Poland and Czechoslovakia (1918); Hungary (1919); Uruguay and Thailand (1932); and Turkey, Brazil and Cuba (1934). In the last days of the conflict or the years immediately following the Second World War, women's suffrage was established in France, Italy and China. In India, the right was introduced in the constitution in 1949, and in Pakistan it was granted in 1956. Swiss women gained the right to vote in federal and most cantonal elections only in 1971. (The country is divided into cantons.) In 1952, the United Nations adopted the Convention on the Political Rights of Women, which held that "women shall be entitled to vote in all elections on equal terms with men, without any discrimination." At present, women do not enjoy voting rights equivalent to those of men in a number of countries, most of which border on the Persian Gulf.

Political Rights for Racial Minorities

The campaign of women for the vote and for the enjoyment of the same rights as men transformed societies. So too did the struggle of minorities for human rights and political rights. In the West, the epochal battle of African Americans against slavery and later against segregation and for the enjoyment of the rights of other Americans has had an immense impact on the United States, indeed on the wider world.

Tension between the so-called slave states in the South and the free states in the North was a fact of life in the United States from the early days of the Union. Political leaders made enormous efforts to prevent the issue of slavery from destroying the Union (and secession by the South). During the 1850s, however, there was a steady march toward the great collision, which came in the following decade. Northerners resented the Fugitive Slave Act, which required them to return runaway slaves to their masters in the South. Although the movement to abolish slavery never won the support of a majority of Americans, the abolitionists grew ever stronger and more insistent in the North.

As the political strains grew more intense, the old political parties, the Democrats and the Whigs, themselves became fractured. In the 1850s, a new party, the Republicans, emerged in the North and the Midwest. While the Republicans did not espouse the abolition of slavery, they were determined to prevent the South's so-called peculiar institution from spreading to new states. Meanwhile in the South, a new political leadership came to the fore made up of men who were intent on defending their region's way of life and the existence of slavery against any challenges.

In the presidential election of 1860, Abraham Lincoln, the Republican candidate, was triumphant. In the election, in which there were four major candidates, although he won a minority of votes, he won enough states and Electoral College votes to become president. In the months following his electoral victory in November

1860 and his inauguration in March 1861, seven states in the Deep South seceded from the Union, and these were soon followed by the secession of six other states, including Virginia, whose capital, Richmond, became the federal capital of the newly created Confederate States of America.

War broke out and it raged for four years. In terms of lives lost, it was the most costly war in American history. The Confederacy fought for its right to secede, and the North fought to sustain the Union. While slavery was not the sole cause of the war, it was a fundamental cause.

On January 1, 1863, the federal government issued the Emancipation Proclamation, an edict that declared "that all persons held as slaves" within the rebellious states "are, and henceforward shall be free." The effect of the proclamation was not to free any slaves in the border states that had remained in the Union or on Confederate territory that had so far been occupied by the Union army, so it did not immediately set anyone free. It did, however, mean that future advances by the Union army would liberate the slaves, and it confirmed that a Union victory in the war would end slavery in the US.[8]

When the war ended with the triumph of the Union in 1865, a brief epoch of rapid reform followed. During the so-called period of Reconstruction, the South was occupied by federal soldiers. Political rights for the recently freed African Americans were on the agenda. In December 1865, the Thirteenth Amendment, which banned slavery, came into force. The Fourteenth Amendment, which came into effect in July 1868, guaranteed the full rights of citizenship to all persons born or naturalized in the US. Its goal was to ensure full rights to the former slaves and to prevent the former states of the Confederacy from enacting legislation to abridge those rights. The last of the so-called Reconstruction Amendments, the fifteenth, came into effect in February 1870. Its goal was to ensure voting rights for the former slaves.

The anticipated spring for African Americans turned out to be a false one, however. It was not many months after the demise of the Confederacy that the repression of blacks in the South began. And it was to last for nearly a century. Despite the constitutional amendments and the efforts of Reconstruction political leaders, the states of the South were soon readmitted to their place in the US Congress. Within those states, new mechanisms to hold the black populations in a position of marginalization and fear were being established. The social elites in the white South saw the stakes as extremely high. In many regions of the South, blacks formed large local majorities of the population. Were they to win political rights, many would be elected to local, state and federal offices, and the power structure would be profoundly altered.

The political party to which the former slaves were wedded was the Republican Party of Lincoln that had emancipated them. For that reason, the whites who were determined to block the emancipation of blacks also targeted activists in the Republican Party. In 1866, the year after the Civil War ended, the Ku Klux Klan was organized in Pulaski, Tennessee, by white supremacists who set out to suppress the freed slaves and rob them of their potential political power. For these whites, the goal was to "sustain the southern way of life."[9]

The few African Americans who held public office in the South during the Reconstruction period were quickly driven from their posts, whether they were elective or appointed. Such an opening for blacks would not come again for a century.[10]

The white Southern establishment created a marginal, miserable world for the black population. For blacks who went to work in the agricultural sector for white owners on cotton or sugar plantations, near slavery or indentured labor was the norm. White owners ran their operations like company towns. They supplied their black tenants or employees with their basic needs — food, clothing, fuel — and charged them more for these goods than they paid them for their labor. The laborers were perennially in debt and as a consequence were obliged to go on working for the owners. The vote, supposedly assured for blacks by the Fifteenth Amendment, was taken away in most of the South through a combination of physical intimidation and the implementation of literacy tests, which they were deemed to have failed however literate they were. Other ways to prohibit blacks from voting were poll taxes and property requirements.

Most of the South became a one-party state where only the Democratic Party was competitive. The real struggles for office took place within the Democratic Party, not between Democrats and Republicans. In the South, prior to the 1960s, the Democratic Party was an all-white party whose members were devoted to the cause of segregation — the creation of a separate realm for blacks that denied them access to the wider society.

Segregation meant that blacks lived apart in their own communities and could not access housing in white communities even if they could afford it. Black education was minimal and far inferior to the education accorded to whites. A crucial US Supreme Court decision in 1896, *Plessy v. Ferguson*, legalized segregation. The case arose as a result of the plaintiff, Plessy, purchasing a first-class rail ticket in Louisiana. Plessy was seven-eighths Caucasian, but under Louisiana law a person whose ancestry was one-eighth African American was deemed to be non-white. Plessy was refused the right to sit in a rail car reserved for whites. The case was fought to the US Supreme Court, which ruled that Plessy's rights were not abridged. It was legal for the state of Louisiana to establish separate arrangements for whites and non-whites, according to the principle of "separate but equal."

Under this legal doctrine, segregation flourished for many more decades. Blacks had to ride in separate rail cars, use separate restroom facilities in public places, ride at the back of buses and in separate spaces on other forms of public transit, and attend all-black schools. They were barred from white recreation facilities.

Attempts on the part of blacks to assert themselves, let alone to protest their condition, were savagely repressed. Lynching of African Americans — a crime committed when a mob of whites assembled to murder individuals, sometimes on the grounds that they had been guilty of some offence, but often on no such pretext — was widespread in the South. According to the Tuskegee Institute, between 1880 and 1951, 3,437 African Americans were lynched, with the frequency of these murders peaking in the late nineteenth century. The most heinous single lynching incident took place in Colfax, Louisiana, in 1873, where 280 African Americans were murdered in what is known as the Colfax Massacre.

While the murders of blacks declined, racial segregation was still in place during the Second World War when the American armed forces were divided into units along racial lines. In Britain, in districts where American troops were based during the conflict, local pubs were required to establish separate times when white or black soldiers could visit. Even though Britain was not racially segregated, the American military required British institutions to go along with these arrangements.

During the 1950s, the first major steps were taken to dismantle segregation in the South. In 1951, a group of parents in Topeka, Kansas, filed a class action suit against the city's board of education on behalf of their children. The suit, filed in the name of one of the plaintiffs, Oliver L. Brown, an African American railroad welder, demanded that the board of education eliminate its policy of racial segregation and allow students to attend the school most convenient to them. The district court ruled in favor of the board of education, citing the Supreme Court ruling in *Plessy v. Ferguson* as its precedent. In 1954, the United States Supreme Court reviewed the case and ruled in favor of Brown.

The historic Supreme Court decision did not overturn the right of private parties to maintain racially segregated restaurants and restrooms. And it did not lead to the immediate desegregation of Southern schools. Most schools in the South were not desegregated until about 1970, and this followed an intense political struggle. The ruling, however, constituted a crucial step toward the achievement of full rights for African Americans.[11]

The end of segregation and the winning of political rights were enormous steps forward for African Americans. These advances were followed, however, by decades of political reaction. White Southerners, formerly solidly loyal to the segregationist wing of the Democratic Party, switched en masse to the Republicans. The rising new right in the US, mostly situated in the Republican Party, launched an assault against the War on Poverty, affirmative action and aid to families with dependent children (all programs that benefited African Americans disproportionately). The first two programs were launched by President Lyndon Johnson in 1964, and the third program dated to the New Deal of the 1930s.

The income and wealth gaps between blacks and other Americans failed to narrow. Blacks also found themselves without much political leverage at the national level. That was because their votes were largely taken for granted by the Democratic Party. And Democrats regarded the so-called soccer moms — white women in the suburbs — as the central demographic in determining the outcomes of elections.

The franchise was a potent weapon, however, if used effectively. In big city contests where African American mayors were elected, the weapon demonstrated its potential. In 2004, a young African American politician from Chicago, Barack Obama, delivered a stirring address at the Democratic National Convention, pointing the way toward a political transformation. In his campaign for his party's presidential nomination in 2008, Obama assembled a formidable coalition of supporters never before brought together by an African American leader. The senator from Illinois was, in many respects, a typical mainstream Democrat with a cautious program and the support of plenty of Big Money backers. His message of change and hope, however, mobilized the young in a fashion not seen since the 1960s. A charismatic leader, Obama revealed that African Americans could now compete effectively for the country's top political job.

Chapter 4
Democracy and the Demise of the Soviet Union

In the late 1980s and early 1990s, in a series of largely peaceful revolutions, the Soviet-backed regimes in Eastern Europe and then the Soviet Union itself disintegrated. Among the millions of people who took to the streets during this remarkable transformation were key elements of civil society, including trade unionists, churchgoers, civil libertarians and intellectuals.

Extraordinary as it may seem to us decades after the fact, the Soviet Union was once understood by millions of people to be the forerunner of a world revolution that would broaden the meaning of democracy for humanity. The Soviet Union was established as a consequence of the Bolshevik (Communist) regime that came to power after the Russian Revolution of November 1917. That revolution was the culmination of struggles for democracy, for the liberation of the peasantry and for socialism that had been underway since the mid-nineteenth century.

In 1905, a great uprising of workers, trade unionists, democrats and socialists pushed the autocratic czarist regime to the brink of collapse. In February 1917, with

Russia reeling from the vast casualties of the First World War and with millions of people suffering from food shortages, the first of the two Russian revolutions of that year erupted, bringing down the regime of Czar Nicholas II. Taking power was Alexander Kerensky, the leader of a shaky coalition of forces dedicated to installing a liberal democratic regime in Russia. The decision of Kerensky's provisional government to sustain Russia's place in the allied military struggle against Germany and Austria-Hungary had fateful consequences. It opened the door to the Bolshevik Revolution in November.

When the Bolsheviks took power under the leadership of Vladimir Ilyich Lenin, Marxists and many other socialists around the world believed this would open the way for the flowering of a democracy that would surpass even the ideals enshrined in the French Revolution and would bring to power, for the first time in history, a regime dedicated to the interests of the working class. Instead, out of the civil war of the early years of the revolution and the political upheavals of the 1920s came a regime ruled by Joseph Stalin, the first secretary of the Communist Party of the Soviet Union. Stalin's totalitarian dictatorship crushed the hopes for democracy.

In the mid 1930s, the Soviet Union adopted a constitution, which on paper was one of the most democratic in the world. Yet although the constitution spelled out the rights of citizens to free speech and assembly and the right to publish what they liked, citizens who tried any of these things did so at their peril. Under Stalin there was no free speech or effective rights to publish or to assemble, even in the top ranks of the Communist Party. Under Stalin's orders, most of the top leaders of the Communist Party, his competitors for power, were arrested and executed.

The Soviet tyranny remained fully in place until Stalin's death in 1953. By that time, the Soviet Union had participated, along with the Western powers, in defeating Nazi Germany in the Second World War. As a consequence of the war, which ended in 1945, the Soviet army occupied almost all of Eastern Europe, including East Germany. Satellite regimes were established in each of these countries and ultimate power rested in Moscow. The citizens of Eastern European countries struggled to regain their freedom from Moscow. East Germans revolted in 1953; Hungarians in 1956; and Czechoslovaks in 1968. In each of these cases, Moscow deployed force to quell the bids for political reform.

In the early 1980s in Poland, a trade union movement named Solidarity was formed under the leadership of Lech Walesa, a worker in the Gdansk shipyards. The movement grew, despite efforts on the part of the Polish government to curtail its influence. In 1989, in partially democratic elections in which a large proportion of seats was reserved for the Communist Party and its allies, Solidarity swept the seats that were genuinely contested and a new government under its leadership was sworn in. In 1990, Lech Walesa was elected president and the following year fully democratic parliamentary elections were held. The Soviet government did not intervene to block these steps toward democracy.

The Soviet government was led by Mikhail Gorbachev, who became general secretary of the Communist Party in 1985. Gorbachev recognized that the Soviet Union was facing a vast economic and social crisis, and that it had fallen far behind the West technologically. He aspired to reforming the Soviet Union economically (perestroika) and allowing a new openness in its politics (glasnost). He believed that such changes would make Communism viable for the future.

From Poland the movements for reform spread to Hungary, East Germany, Czechoslovakia and other Eastern European states, as well as to the Soviet Union itself. In the summer of 1989, the Hungarian government decided that it would not block the passage of people out of the country to the West. Tens of thousands of Eastern Europeans poured through this hole in the once-solid Iron Curtain after traveling to Hungary for their annual vacations. There they boarded trains that transported them to Austria. In East Germany, a movement for democratic reform took shape, focused on major churches in Leipzig, East Berlin and other cities. Opponents of the regime took to the streets in ever larger peaceful demonstrations.

Under the influence of Gorbachev in Moscow, the Communist regimes in the region did not crack down on the movements for change. The local military and police and above all, the Soviet Red Army, did not intervene as they had in the past in the face of opposition. That the changed policy about the use of force did not apply to all Communist regimes was made tragically clear in Beijing in June 1989. There thousands of people who sought democratic change occupied Tiananmen Square in the heart of the Chinese capital. For a number of days it appeared that peaceful change might be possible in China as well as in Eastern Europe. When the first units of the Chinese military were dispatched to end the occupation of the square, soldiers fraternized with the demonstrators and the scene remained peaceful. Then came deadly force. New units were dispatched to the square. Hundreds of protestors were killed and hundreds more were rounded up and imprisoned. Some were never heard from again.

In East Germany, matters came to a head in the autumn of 1989. Mikhail Gorbachev visited East Berlin to participate in the celebration of the fortieth anniversary of the founding of the German Democratic Republic. He met with Eric Honecker, the hard-line dictator at the head of the East German regime. It was clear at their meeting that they did not see eye to eye.

Honecker had presided for nearly three decades over a brutal state that cracked down on any show of opposition, banning the publication of writings critical of the regime or the performance of plays that did not conform to Communist orthodoxy. At the center of the regime's repressive apparatus was the Stasi, the East German secret police, whose units collected and kept files on tens of thousands of citizens. (Those files have been preserved and are now open to citizens who wish to review the records the Stasi kept of them, their associates and their families.) A crucial tool of repression was the Berlin wall, constructed under the direction of Eric Honecker in 1961. The wall, which divided East Berlin from West Berlin, was built to staunch the flow of tens of thousands of East Germans each year to the western city. (With the wall in place, the price of flight was often death — 171 people were killed or died trying to escape to the West from the day the wall went up in August 1961 to November 1989.)

As the protests swelled in size — in Leipzig from 70,000 people to 300,000 people a week later and then to close to a million — the East German regime tried desperately to save itself. Rumors spread that Eric Honecker had ordered security forces to open fire on demonstrators. Completely discredited, the leader was ousted from the Politburo, the top decision-making body of the East German Communist Party, in mid-October. The new leader was the former security chief, Egon Krenz, who claimed to be a reformer in the manner of Mikhail Gorbachev and promised change and dialogue.

Krenz could not stem the growing demand for free elections and freedom to travel, however. On November 9, 1989, in response to orders from above, the East German border guards allowed East Berliners to flood through Checkpoint Charlie, the gate in the wall that separated East Berlin from its western counterpart. When word spread that the wall was open, tens of thousands of people flooded into West Berlin. Remarkable scenes of joy and celebration followed on both sides of the border.

It was the symbolic end of the Communist regime, and the legal end was not long in coming. On November

9, Berliners began demolishing the wall. Enterprising young men and women equipped with hammers and chisels chipped pieces out of the wall, selling them to passersby for one or two Deutsch marks (about $2 to $3 at the time).[1] A few months after the opening of the wall, East Germans decided in a referendum that they wished to join the Federal Republic of Germany. In July 1990, the East German currency, the ostmark, was replaced by the West German Deutsch mark, with Easterners receiving a highly favorable rate of exchange for their holdings in the old currency. In early October 1990, political union followed. East Germany was no more. As citizens of the Federal Republic of Germany, the 17 million East Germans gained full political rights.

They faced a long and difficult period of economic and social adjustment, however. To bring the population, infrastructure and economic base of the former East Germany up to the standards of the West, the Federal Republic invested tens of billions of Deutsch marks in the region. The unemployment rate in the former East Germany was, and still is, considerably higher than in the West. Many in Western Germany resented the tax bill for the reconstruction of the East, and many in the East took exception to what they saw as the condescension of Westerners. But Germany had become one again, and for the first time since Hitler's ascension to power in 1933, all Germans enjoyed full democratic rights.

The opening of the Berlin wall heralded the collapse of the other Eastern European regimes. Within a few weeks, tens of thousands of people took to the streets of

Prague and other Czechoslovak cities and carried out their own Velvet Revolution, as it came to be known for its nonviolent achievement of change. The leading figure in the drive for democracy in Czechoslovakia was the writer and dissident Václav Havel, who had spent time in prison for writings critical of the Communist regime.[2]

In the years prior to the Velvet Revolution, Havel and other writers reproduced their works using primitive printing devices and distributed them to tiny audiences of a few dozen people. Now the tide of history had turned in their favor.

Change swept through Hungary as well during these weeks. The Communist government announced that democratic multiparty elections would be held in March 1990. Although Communists contested these elections, they fared poorly and a new government came to office.[3]

In December 1989, the movement for change swept out the dictatorial Rumanian regime of Nicolae Ceausescu. Following a brief firefight in the capital, Bucharest, the forces of the dictator stood down and the militias of those seeking change seized control, capturing Ceausescu in the process. Once in power, they mounted a summary trial, found Ceausescu guilty and took the former leader and his wife outside and shot them.

Meanwhile in the Soviet Union itself, the old order was crumbling. In Moscow, the drive for democracy brought Boris Yeltsin, a maverick Communist Party member and advocate of reform, to the fore. Having won elections in the Russian Federation (by far the largest of the fifteen Soviet Republics) in June 1991, Yeltsin became president of Russia. Western powers began treating him as the real leader of the country. Gorbachev held onto the increasingly shaky post of president of the Soviet Union. In August, in a botched coup d'état, dissident hard-line elements in the Soviet government made a desperate bid to reverse the course of political reform. The coup leaders issued an emergency decree banning political activity and the publication of most Russian newspapers. Armed units surrounded Gorbachev's dacha on the Black Sea and held the Soviet president prisoner in his holiday retreat.

In Moscow, the leaders of the coup attempted to arrest Boris Yeltsin, but thousands of his supporters went into the streets to safeguard the office of the Russian leader. After three days, the coup collapsed. In the process, power flowed to Yeltsin, and Gorbachev was rendered politically impotent. During the autumn of 1991, the Russian government took over the ministries of the Soviet government, and the governments of the other republics began to do the same thing. In December, the final collapse was precipitated by the results of a referendum in Ukraine, the second-most populous of the republics, in which over 90 percent of voters chose the option of political independence. On December 25, recognizing that the collapse was irreversible, Gorbachev resigned as Soviet president and handed over all of his powers to Boris Yeltsin. The following day, the Supreme Soviet dissolved itself and on December 31, all remaining functions of the Soviet regime ceased, having been assumed by the member republics. With the exception of the three Baltic states, Latvia, Lithuania and Estonia, the former republics of the Soviet Union joined the Commonwealth of Independent States (CIS), a relatively powerless new federation in which real sovereignty was exercised by the member states. For all practical purposes the CIS has been a non-entity.

The collapse of the Soviet Union and its Eastern European satellites is a sharp reminder of the transitory nature of governing arrangements. A great state that had vied for power with the United States for more than forty years during the Cold War disappeared as a consequence, not of military collapse or outside invasion, but of a political, social and economic crisis that was hardly visible to outside observers. A vast realm, with a population of 300 million people, ceased to live under Soviet-style Communism. Most of the newly created independent states quickly moved to systems in which multiparty elections were featured. The shift to democracy was highly uneven, however, and was much more successful in some cases than in others.

A remarkable feature of the breakup of the Soviet Union and its empire was the relative nonviolence of this immense historical transformation. Almost without exception, the successor regimes recognized the established borders among the former Soviet Republics and among the Eastern European countries.

The inhabitants of another multiethnic state that fell to pieces during these years were not so fortunate, however. The nationalist impulses that were at work in the Soviet Union tore Communist Yugoslavia (not under

Moscow domination) asunder. Vicious wars were fought between the Serbs and the Croats, the Serbs and the Bosnians, and finally the Serbs and the largely Albanian population of Kosovo. Tens of thousands of people died. The savage struggles included massacres of civilian populations, ethnic cleansing and systematic rape.

North Atlantic Treaty Organization (NATO) troops were dispatched to Bosnia but were ineffective for a long time in halting the fighting around Sarajevo. In 1999, NATO intervened in Kosovo, launching an air war against Serbian forces that included the bombing of the Serbian capital of Belgrade. Kosovo remains occupied by NATO troops. In 2008, Kosovo proclaimed its independence from Serbia, and the new state was recognized as sovereign by the United States and the member states of the European Union. Serbia denounced the move and was supported by Russia in its refusal to recognize Kosovo's independence.[4]

The component parts of the former Yugoslavia have established multiparty electoral systems and competitive elections, but the progress toward full democracy in the Balkans has been slow, with frequent setbacks.

While the Eastern European countries that were formerly in the Soviet sphere have moved toward the status of full democracies — a process solidified by the accession of these countries to the European Union — the former Soviet republics have followed a more precarious course.

In Russia, with its population of 140 million people, the progress toward democracy was only partial, and in recent years, the country has slid back in the direction of authoritarian government. The Yeltsin years were chaotic and were followed by the election of Vladimir Putin, Yeltsin's hand-picked successor, as president in 2000 and then again in 2004. It soon became clear that Putin, a former career KGB (Soviet secret police) operative, was no committed democrat. Under Putin's rule, Russian economic growth resumed, largely as a consequence of rising petroleum prices and the increasing export of Russian oil and natural gas to Western Europe. In March 2008, Dmitri Medvedev, a Putin protégé, easily won the Russian presidential election. When he was sworn in as president two months later, Medvedev's first act was to nominate Putin as prime minister.

As elsewhere in Eastern Europe, the transition to a market economy and private enterprise has been marred by a widening gap between a small wealthy class at the top and the rest of the population. At the lower end, much of the population has sunk into destitution. An irony, in Russia as well as in Eastern Europe, is that a high proportion of the first capitalists were former Communist bureaucrats. Those with the best societal connections were often able to manage a head start for themselves in the new system.

The new regimes in Eastern Europe and the former Soviet Union received plenty of advice from the West, especially from economists, about how to manage their shift from command economies, in which the state made most basic planning decisions, to market economies, in which private corporations would account for most economic activity. Much of the advice that was initially heeded came from economists influenced by the approach of thinkers at the University of Chicago, whose most illustrious proponent was Milton Friedman, the father of monetarism. The advice was that the new regimes should move rapidly to privatize state-owned firms; open their doors to outside investment; end subsidies to citizens for food, housing and education; and end the widespread provision of employment by the state.

In Russia, during the first decade after the demise of the Soviet Union, the conditions of life for the majority deteriorated. Millions of people suffered a lack of health care, housing, education and diet, despite the opening of lavish establishments for the newly rich and the rapidly rising price of real estate in Moscow. Alcoholism became a national epidemic. The average life expectancy, especially that of men, declined appreciably, from sixty-two years in 1980 to fifty-eight years in 1999.[5] Embedded in the emerging private sector economy was a new criminal class. Organized crime flourished, taking root in the legitimate economy, and Russian criminal syndicates made their presence felt in many parts of the world.

The miserable lives of ordinary people have improved somewhat in recent years, although much of the economic growth fed the wealth of Russia's new billionaires with their conspicuously opulent lifestyles. Putin revived the power of the Russian state, pushing out private companies whose chief executives he regarded as rivals, and even jailing them, while boosting state ownership and control in the crucial petroleum sector. In 2003, Mikhail Khodorkovsky, the wealthy and powerful chief executive of Yukos Oil, was arrested and sentenced to an eight-year prison term for tax evasion and other financial irregularities. His company was then broken up, and many of its assets were acquired by Rosneft, the state-owned petroleum company.

Media outlets declined in number and genuine diversity. Opponents of Putin received little coverage for their political activities. By the time Putin was re-elected in 2004, Russia was lurching back toward the status of a one-party state. Rallies and public demonstrations on behalf of opposition political leaders were often broken up by the police or by pro-Putin hooligans. Russia was reasserting itself as an economic and military power, but the sun was setting on its brief and chaotic era of pluralism and democracy.

Meanwhile in Ukraine, pro-democracy advocates were locked in a struggle against the forces of a renewed authoritarianism. In late 2004 and early 2005, a mass movement focused on the capital, Kiev, protested the results of the presidential election in which widespread corruption, vote rigging and intimidation had delivered victory to the sitting prime minister Viktor Yanukovych. Hundreds of thousands of people, clad in orange, braved the cold in enormous demonstrations in Independence Square to demand new elections and to promote the cause of the other major candidate in the elections, Viktor Yushchenko. Yushchenko had been the victim of a politically motivated dioxide-poisoning assault that altered his facial appearance and left him with long-term pain and permanent health problems.

The political stalemate was broken by the Ukrainian Supreme Court, which invalidated the election results on the grounds that they had involved extensive electoral fraud. New runoff elections were called for December 26, 2004. The results favored Yushchenko, who was declared the winner by the Supreme Court and was inaugurated on January 23, 2005, in front of hundreds of thousands of his followers.

This new pro-Western government soon disillusioned many of its supporters, however. Change came too slowly for those who had filled the streets during the Orange Revolution. Moreover, the struggle within Ukraine was no simple contest between democrats and authoritarians. In recent years outside interests, both Western and Russian, have intervened in the contest for control of Ukraine — the Westerners trying to pull the country toward Europe, the Russians attempting to keep Ukraine close to Moscow.

As president, Yushchenko showed himself to be as willing to skirt democratic rules as his rival Yanukovych had been. A major player has been Yulia Tymoshenko, a businesswoman who became wealthy in the petroleum industry and who was centrally involved in the Orange Revolution. She was named prime minister by Yushchenko. Since then the power struggles have continued and while Tymoshenko, who sometimes appears pro-Western and sometimes pro-Russian, was prime minister in 2008, it was not clear which of the factions would emerge supreme.

Along the southern rim of the former Soviet Union,

the independent successor states are caught in internal political struggles as well as being pressured to become client states of the great powers — the United States, Russia and China. Kazakhstan and Azerbaijan, significant petroleum-producing countries, have been pulled into the American sphere, with their oil and natural gas production geared for exports to the West. The state of Georgia is a political battleground. And in southern Russia itself, a violent civil struggle is being waged in Chechnya between local forces seeking secession from Russia and the Russian state.

In all of these cases, the aspirations of the population for democracy are endangered by the force of outside powers in pursuit of their strategic goals.

Chapter 5
Movements for Democracy in the Developing World

During the first decade of the twenty-first century, while the energy of democratic movements and parties has by no means been exhausted in the West, the locus of democratic struggles has shifted to the South. Arguably, the future global status of democracy will depend on the outcome of developments there.

Latin America
Living under the domination of the United States and of American and multinational corporate interests, Latin America's struggles against colonialism and for democracy have continued long after most of the region was liberated from Spanish rule in the first decades of the nineteenth century. Latin America is a classic case of long-term alliances between local landowners and business interests, the military and ruling political cliques, and American political and business interests. This pervasive pattern has stood in the way of social and economic advance and the permanent victory of democratic forces. Struggles for land reform (to transfer land from the great

landowners to the peasants), for the organization of workers into unions, and for honest government that serves the majority of the people have waxed and waned in Latin America for the past century and a half.

For long periods, as during the height of the Cold War between the United States and the Soviet Union, American power was amassed against movements for basic reform. In 1954, acting on behalf of the US-based United Fruit Company, the American Central Intelligence Agency sponsored a coup against the reform-minded government of Guatemala. After the Cuban Revolution led by Fidel Castro triumphed in Havana, the Kennedy administration sponsored a military assault on Cuba by anti-Castro dissidents in the spring of 1961. In the aftermath of the failure of the Bay of Pigs operation, the US government feared the spread of Castroism throughout Latin America. Washington redoubled its efforts to maintain close ties to political rulers and the military across the region, preferring authoritarian regimes to movements for democratic change. When Socialist Salvador Allende won the presidency of Chile in 1970 in a democratic election, the Nixon administration was alarmed at the prospect of sweeping change in that country. In September 1973, Allende was killed when a coup d'état led by General Augusto Pinochet installed a right-wing dictatorship that murdered hundreds more of its political foes and imprisoned thousands. Washington supported the Pinochet regime from day one. The new Chilean government received copious advice from right-wing economists at the University of Chicago, who drew up plans for a harshly conservative market-centered economic order in which social programs were slashed and trade unions were cast aside.

In recent years, there has been a powerful resurgence of democracy and democratic movements throughout Latin America. Following the demise of the Pinochet dictatorship, Chile has firmly re-established itself as a democracy, reconnecting with the democratic heritage that long predated the military coup in 1973. The crimes of the dictatorship have been investigated and its victims compensated. Argentina and Brazil, nations with frequent despotic chapters in their past, have established functioning multiparty political systems with free and fair elections.

The new driving force on the continent is Venezuela, whose oil wealth allowed its left-wing government to challenge the power of the US, not only within its own borders, but throughout Latin America. The struggle for power in Venezuela between the old establishment and the government led by the president, left-wing populist Hugo Chávez, was fiercely waged. In 2002, an attempted coup against Chávez toppled him for forty-eight hours before his supporters filled the streets of Caracas and restored him to power. Chávez fought for greater state control of Venezuela's petroleum industry and established programs to aid the poor in the wretched barrios on the edge of the capital, his key base of support.

Chávez is constantly accused of scheming to create a dictatorship. In 2007, his government sponsored a referendum with the goal of changing the country's constitution to allow the president to run for a third term of office. When Chávez lost the referendum, he accepted his defeat, insisting though that he would push ahead with his program of radical social reform.

Of enormous significance was the rise of a powerful reform movement in Bolivia led by Evo Morales, who won the nation's presidential election in 2005 with 53.7 percent of the popular vote. A Bolivian of indigenous origin whose political base was centered on the indigenous population in the Andean regions of the country, Morales came to power on a program of sweeping economic and social reform. His goal was to vastly improve the quality of life for the nation's indigenous people and the poor. Morales' program brought him into sharp conflict with the local business elite as well as US corporations and the US government. It included the transfer of control of natural gas, oil and other mineral resources from the private sector to the Bolivian state and people; agrarian reform; and the establishment of new institutions to revitalize Bolivian democracy to make it serve those who had been left out in the past.

It was not long before Bolivia's traditional elites organized themselves to blunt the effectiveness of the Morales government, and in the summer of 2008 they sponsored a national referendum to remove the president from office. The move to oust the president was rejected by a resounding 67.7 percent of voters, however. Morales managed in the recall struggle to win support that ranged far beyond his traditional political base.

In Mexico, after decades of rule by a single political

party, the PRI (Institutional Revolutionary Party), the country evolved into a multiparty democracy. Over the course of several decades, the grip of the PRI was loosened. In 2000, with the election of Vicente Fox of the National Action Party as Mexico's president, the PRI's hold on the country's top job for seventy-one years came to an end. Although corruption is omnipresent both in Mexican politics and in the administration of the state at all levels, the country has made giant strides toward a genuine democracy in which major shades of political opinion from right to left are available to voters.

In other regions of the world, the forces of democracy found themselves embroiled in struggles whose outcomes were, at best, uncertain.

The Middle East and North Africa
In the Middle East, with its enormous geo-strategic significance due to its holdings of over 60 percent of the world's proven petroleum reserves, democracy is more fugitive. Although Israel makes a plausible claim to being the region's only full-fledged democracy, its occupation of much of the West Bank and its strategic dominance of the West Bank and Gaza means that Israeli democracy applies only to Israelis, leaving Palestinians effectively marginalized and stateless.

As for the other states in the region, including Egypt, Sudan, Algeria, Lebanon, Saudi Arabia, Kuwait, Syria and Iran, not one comes close to being a genuine democracy. In the cases of Egypt and Algeria, regimes have refused to hold free and fair elections because they fear that parties dedicated to the creation of Islamic republics will be the winners.

The Palestinians constitute a very particular case — a people fighting for a homeland, having suffered occupation for over four decades. There has been a democratic impulse in Palestinian politics, but this has often been nullified by armed struggles between factions whose rivalries have turned, among other things, on which faction has been most successful in launching suicide terrorist attacks on Israel. The history of the major factions, the Palestinian Liberation Organization and Hamas, has been dramatically influenced by the interference of foreign states and actors. The secular PLO, founded by Yasir Arafat, which became the main party devoted to the struggle against Israel, was later challenged by Hamas, a militant Islamist faction. Ironically, Hamas was founded with secret support from the Israelis and the Americans, their goal being to split the Palestinians and to build the strength of a right-wing religious movement to counter the secular and left-leaning PLO.

Later when the PLO adopted a less confrontational approach, Hamas became the more implacable foe of Israel, which prompted the US and Israel to align more closely to the PLO after the death of Arafat. When Hamas won parliamentary elections for the Palestinian Authority in the West Bank and Gaza in January 2006, the US and the EU responded to the democratic choice of the Palestinian people by sharply cutting funding to the Authority. The PLO and Hamas resorted to armed conflict to resolve their own struggle for control. As a consequence, the PLO ended up in charge of the West Bank and Hamas gained control of Gaza. The Western powers and Israel pursued negotiations with the PLO, the goal being to resolve the Palestinian question, while leaving Hamas isolated in Gaza. The Western powers poured aid into the West Bank and left Gaza destitute and subject to the harsh conditions of an Israeli blockade. Israel justified the blockade as retaliation for the launching of rockets against communities in Israel by militants based in Gaza.

The case of Iraq is a special one. It is important to distinguish between genuine struggles for democracy and the use of the idea of democracy to rally support for military or political struggles whose underlying objectives have little or nothing to do with it. The 2003 invasion of Iraq by the United States and a coalition of other states highlights this distinction.

The Bush administration's stated rationale for the invasion was that it was essential to pre-empt the deployment of weapons of mass destruction against the US or its allies by the regime of Saddam Hussein. From the first days of the assault against Iraq, a key proclaimed US goal was to overthrow the dictatorial Iraqi government and to replace it with a democratic regime dedicated to the rule of law and respect for human rights. When it became apparent several months after the invasion that Iraq possessed no weapons of mass destruction, the rationale that democracy was the goal of the continuing war grew ever more central. The choices were stark according to the Bush administration: US failure in Iraq would strengthen al Qaeda and Iran and would worsen the global terrorist threat, while US success would advance the cause of democracy throughout the Middle East.

Six years after the invasion, hundreds of thousands of Iraqis have been killed and an estimated 2.2 million people have fled the country. While an elected government is in place, the country has effectively been partitioned into Shiite, Sunni and Kurdish zones run by sectarian militias and political factions. As for the cause of human rights, in most of the country, Iraqi women are much more subject to fundamentalist Islamic rule that limits their lifestyle and occupational choices and dictates their manner of dress than had been the case prior to the invasion.

Dressing up the US invasion in democratic garb can be likened to the West's nineteenth-century habit of pointing to the presence of missionaries alongside warriors, businessmen and government officials as a way to justify imperial forays in African and Asian countries.

Asia

In Asia, which is home to 60 percent of the world's population, democracy is firmly established in some crucially important states. With a billion people, India is the world's most populous democracy and has had a multiparty parliamentary system since 1947. Democracy in India, however, has frequently been compromised by violent religious conflicts involving Hindus, Muslims and Sikhs; by the periodic breakdown of state governments; by the impoverished state of more than half of the population and by the assassination of political leaders. That said, the success of democracy in India has been a crucial factor in the country's rise as a technologically advanced economic power and the site of a cultural sector with worldwide influence.

On the other hand, as China becomes a power capable of challenging the global sway of the United States, it remains a one-party state. Challenges to Communist Party rule or attempts to promote religious practices not sanctioned by the state are met with violent repression, arrest and stiff prison sentences. In 1997, China successfully absorbed Hong Kong (which had been a British crown colony for a century) and allowed the city to retain its capitalist economy. (In practice, all of China has a state capitalist economic system.) Hong Kong's press freedom continues as does a degree of competitive politics. The members of the governing administration in Hong Kong are mostly appointed by Beijing, however, and the city's government is firmly under the control of the Chinese state.

China is determined to win back control of Taiwan, which it claims as its territory. While Taiwan has a multiparty political system, any move on the part of the government in Taipei to declare independence from China would precipitate a grave crisis. Beijing has threatened war in such a situation. The United States, Taiwan's military protector, recognizes the island as a part of China but insists that any future unification must be non-coerced.

Japan, the Asian economic mega-power, with living standards that are among the highest in the world, has been a democracy since its postwar constitution came into effect in 1947. Although the country has a multiparty electoral system, a single party, the Liberal Democratic Party (LDP), has dominated every government for the past five decades. A consequence of the LDP's role is that much of the decisive political conflict in Japan takes place among the factions and leaders of the party, meaning there is a lack of transparency at the top level of Japanese politics.

Two other major Asian nations, Pakistan and Indonesia, have had episodes of democratic government, but for long periods of time these states have been ruled by military dictatorships. Pakistan, formed at the same time as India with the end of British rule in 1947, has been a state in which political parties, with the support of large sections of the middle classes, including lawyers and elements of the judiciary, have struggled to establish a functioning multiparty democracy. Other contenders for power have been Islamist factions that are determined to make Pakistan an Islamic republic and the military, which has consistently been the most powerful institution in the country.

The most recent chapter in the political history of Pakistan began in 1999 when General Pervez Musharraf seized power and ruled for almost a decade as the head of a government in which the constitution and parliamentary elections were suspended. While the US initially protested this assault on democracy and cut financial aid to the country, the administration of President George W. Bush relented when Musharraf declared his support for the US War on Terror and the American invasion of Afghanistan following the September 11, 2001, terror attacks on New York and Washington DC.

In the autumn of 2007, Musharraf declared that he was committed to return Pakistan to the status of a constitutional democracy. Two major opposition political leaders, Nawaz Sharif, of the Pakistan Muslim League, and Benazir Bhutto, of the Pakistan People's Party, returned to Pakistan from foreign exile to lead their parties into parliamentary elections. (Sharif first returned in September 2007, only to be forced back into exile, and then re-entered Pakistan two months later and was permitted to stay in the country.)

In October 2007, while remaining in uniform, Musharraf proceeded to contest an election for the country's presidency, although it was unclear whether the judges would let the election result stand. The election for the country's top post was held in Pakistan's two houses of parliament and in four provincial assemblies. In this electoral college contest, Musharraf won all but five votes in the two houses of parliament and swept the ballots in the provincial assemblies with huge majorities.

The political maneuvering was a part of Musharraf's attempt to re-establish civilian rule with himself as president. On November 3, 2007, President Musharraf declared a state of emergency. He suspended Pakistan's constitution, fired the chief justice of the Supreme Court, Iftikhar Muhammad Chaudhry, and lined the streets of Islamabad, the capital, with police officers. There were a number of motives behind Musharraf's desperate move.

For one thing, he faced the real possibility that the Supreme Court would nullify his election to the presidency prior to his stepping down as head of the armed forces. Musharraf's crackdown was aimed widely at the judiciary and the country's leading lawyers, the centers from which arguments against his election as president were being mounted. Thousands of lawyers and judges were among those rounded up and imprisoned. In addition to the threat from lawyers and the judiciary, Musharraf was facing political challenges from a number of quarters.

To the United States and other Western countries, Musharraf explained the state of emergency as a measure aimed at fighting terrorism and extremism. While US Secretary of State Condoleezza Rice was quick to condemn Musharraf's move and to demand a "quick return to constitutional law," the US was more fearful of a collapse into chaos in Pakistan than it was of martial law. A week after his proclaimed emergency, Musharraf told Pakistanis in a televised address that he planned to step down as head of the armed forces and to end the suspension of the constitution as soon as possible. He announced that parliamentary elections scheduled for January 2008 would take place despite the imposition of emergency rule.

On December 27, 2007, Benazir Bhutto died at the hands of assassins in the streets of Rawalpindi, following an address to her supporters there. Her death unleashed a wave of unrest in Pakistan, gravely deepening the crisis of legitimacy faced by the regime. Parliamentary elections were delayed until mid-February 2008, when Musharraf's party was dealt a devastating defeat. Pakistanis cast their ballots largely in favor of the parties of the late Ms. Bhutto and Mr. Sharif. President Musharraf swore in a new coalition government to serve under him with Yousaf Raza Gilani, of the Pakistan People's Party, as prime minister. Soon though, Musharraf's position grew untenable. Facing the likelihood of impeachment, the president resigned in August 2008. Days later, federal and provincial parliaments elected Asif Ali Zardari, the leader of the Pakistan People's Party and the widower of Benazir Bhutto, as the country's new president.

The postwar history of Indonesia (Asia's third-most populous country with over 200 million inhabitants) has mainly been a succession of dictatorships. Sukarno, the leader of the country's struggle for independence from Dutch colonial rule, held power as president from 1945 to 1967. The Sukarno years involved shifting political alliances in the country and a transition of Indonesia toward dictatorship. While the country was initially a Western-style democracy, at least in principle, Sukarno claimed that this system of government was not appropriate and argued instead for what he called "guided democracy." The Indonesian leader developed close ties to the Soviet Union and China, and received large supplies of arms from these powers. To prevent the country from being drawn into the Soviet bloc, the US government increased its own provision of munitions to Indonesia.

In 1965, in a chaotic period of struggle in Indonesia involving pro- and anti-Communist factions, Major General Suharto emerged as the country's strongman and initiated a purge of Communist Party members and supporters and a crackdown against ethnic Chinese due to the economic power they wielded. Over the next year, about half a million people were slaughtered in what an official CIA report described as "one of the worst mass murders of the twentieth century."[1] Sukarno's power was sharply reduced as a consequence of the violence unleashed by the military. In a series of steps, the president's authority was stripped away until he was removed from office and placed under house arrest in 1967, where he remained until his death in 1970.

Suharto succeeded Sukarno as president in 1968 and aligned his country with the Western powers, developing strong economic ties with the West and opening Indonesia to a wave of foreign investment. Suharto's dictatorial regime held power by maintaining a strong military and by developing an effective intelligence apparatus whose role was to keep a lid on any attempts to promote political alternatives. Although the regime made a show of holding presidential elections, only a few political parties, those handpicked by Suharto, were allowed to participate.

In 1975, following the overthrow of the Salazar dictatorship in Portugal and the subsequent removal of Portuguese soldiers from the former colony of East Timor, Suharto dispatched Indonesian troops, opening a prolonged occupation of the territory. The Indonesian government declared that East Timor had become Indonesia's twenty-seventh province. As political movements in East Timor struggled for independence, Indonesia responded with extreme brutality, and over the next quarter century 200,000 people were killed.

Following a political arrangement reached among the United States, Indonesia and Portugal, a referendum sponsored by the United Nations was held in East Timor in 1999. By an overwhelming majority the people of the territory chose the option of independence. From 1999 to 2002, a UN transitional administrator worked with local political formations to guide East Timor toward full national sovereignty, which was achieved in 2002, when the new country became a member of the United Nations.

Suharto remained in power until May 1998, when he was forced to resign following two years of increasing protests and rioting in opposition to his dictatorial regime. The last chaotic years of the Suharto dictatorship followed the rebuilding of left-wing and working-class movements whose goals were to oppose the exploitation of Indonesian labor. Among the factors contributing to Suharto's loss of popularity was the widespread cronyism and corruption of his regime. The dictator's friends and family were enriched while ordinary people were scarcely paid for their labor.

The removal of Suharto from power opened an era in which features of democratic rule were established. In 2004, Susilo Bambang Yudhoyono was elected president of Indonesia in a direct popular election.

In Burma (Myanmar), one of the world's most closely

watched struggles for democracy has been underway. In the early 1990s, following several decades of repressive military rule, a movement for democracy under the inspired leadership of Nobel Peace Prize winner Aung San Sui Kyi demanded political change. Sui Kyi is the leader of the National League for Democracy Party and should have become prime minister of Burma following the victory of her party in national elections in 1990. In a speech in which she made the case for democracy, she declared: "It is not power that corrupts but fear. Fear of losing power corrupts those who wield it and fear of the scourge of power corrupts those who are subject to it."[2]

While Sui Kyi has been free for brief intervals, she has also been imprisoned and has spent long periods living under house arrest, with the regime sharply restricting her access to delegations wishing to visit her. In August 2007, protests in opposition to the junta's decision to allow fuel prices to rise sharply were quickly repressed. The following month, however, when new protests were mounted, this time led by Buddhist monks, who have immense prestige in Burma, the regime briefly allowed them to take place. When the numbers in the streets swelled into the tens of thousands, however, the junta cracked down. After issuing warnings to the demonstrators, troops viciously attacked the crowds, and an undetermined number of protestors were killed and many savagely beaten. Some Buddhist monks were among the dead. Security forces raided Buddhist monasteries and arrested hundreds of monks to spearhead their assault on the organizers of the protests.

When Cyclone Nargis devastated the Irrawaddy Delta in May 2008, close to 150,000 people died as a consequence of the storm and its aftermath. Determined to put its own survival ahead of all else, the Burmese junta lost precious time blocking and limiting the receipt of aid to the cyclone's survivors, thereby dramatically increasing the death toll.

Africa

Africa, the second-most populous continent, is home to 900 million people. The forty-eight countries located in sub-Saharan Africa (North Africa's politics are closely tied to that of the Middle East), despite a wide diversity of social, economic, religious and cultural settings, find themselves facing a "remarkably similar predicament" as historian Gerald Caplan has written.[3] Throughout this vast region, "underdevelopment, conflict, famine, AIDS, [and] wretched governance" are all too common, Caplan says. There have been, as well, however, important movements for democracy on the continent.

In recent decades, the transformative democratic movement in Africa was the struggle against apartheid in South Africa. South Africa has a population of 44 million people, about 80 percent of whom are black. Whites, who make up just over 9 percent of the population, are divided into two major groups — Afrikaners, descended from immigrants from Holland in the seventeenth century, and those descended from British immigrants.

From the time of the arrival of the Afrikaners in South Africa, black Africans were treated as an inferior people.

Following the victory of the Afrikaner-dominated Nationalist Party in elections in 1948, the South African government implemented a full-fledged state system based on race known as apartheid, meaning "apartness" in Afrikaans. The state drew up precise definitions (absurd as these were) of the four racial groups into which the population was divided — "whites," "Bantus" (blacks), "coloreds" (mixed race) and "Asians." Rights in the country were based on a person's racial status. Under the system, the population was placed in a pyramid with whites at the top, blacks at the bottom and the other two groups in between. In addition to political rights — blacks had no right to vote in national elections, while coloreds and Asians had limited voting rights at times — race determined where people could travel and the activities in which they could engage. Transportation systems, restaurants, hotels and swimming facilities were strictly segregated on the basis of race.

The struggle against apartheid was waged within South Africa, and increasingly from the outside. The most important political movement fighting to overturn the system was the African National Congress (ANC). The South African government responded to resisters with vicious repression, gunning down demonstrators, as in the Sharpeville massacre in March 1960, when sixty-nine protesters were killed, including eight women and ten children, and more than 180 were injured. The regime also killed leaders of the movement, such as Steve Biko, the anti-apartheid activist who was brutally murdered while in police custody in September 1977.

The most esteemed leader of the ANC was Nelson Mandela, who spent twenty-seven years in prison. Over time, Mandela's political outlook evolved from the advocacy of violent revolution to a belief in nonviolent resistance in keeping with the thought of Mahatma (meaning "great soul") Gandhi, whose own political career began in South Africa. From behind bars, Mandela sought a fundamental political and economic transformation in South Africa that would include the reconciliation of whites with the African majority.

As pressure mounted in opposition to apartheid around the world, South Africa was excluded from the Commonwealth, as well as from the Olympic Games and other international sporting events, and became the target of an increasingly effective economic boycott of the country's exports. In February 1990, Mandela was released from prison. Apartheid crumbled when a section of the Afrikaner leadership decided that the system was no longer sustainable. A few days before Mandela's release, South African president F.W. de Klerk ended the ban on the ANC and other organizations involved in the struggle.

Freed from prison, Mandela resumed his active leadership of the ANC. Over the next four years, he presided over the ANC's side in the negotiations with the government that led to elections in 1994 in which all adults — black, colored, Asian, white — could participate. On May 10, 1994, Mandela was inaugurated as South African president, with former president de Klerk serving as his first deputy in a national unity government. Mandela and de Klerk were the joint recipients of the Nobel Peace Prize in 1993.

The post-apartheid government investigated the crimes committed by the former all-white regime, but the goal was reconciliation on the basis of a full accounting of the wrongs of the past rather than the punishment of the wrongdoers. While this process was remarkably successful considering the passions on all sides, what has been intractably difficult has been achieving basic economic and social change. In principle, all South Africans now live in a democracy in which they enjoy equal rights. Although an educated, politically powerful African elite has emerged, and some black Africans have entered the country's wealthy class, the country remains fundamentally divided between whites and the majority of the population on the basis of income and wealth. South Africa functions in the world economy with a market system that welcomes foreign investment and operates according to the norms of the private sector. Although the achievements of the South African movement for democracy have been enormous, providing a beacon of hope for peoples around the world, a great distance remains to be traveled before the country becomes a full democracy in which the life chances of citizens are no longer deeply skewed as a consequence of the legacy of the past, and therefore, of race.

In the other countries in sub-Saharan Africa, democracy and human rights conditions vary, but the broad picture is far from positive. To a considerable extent, the history of European colonialism and the process of decolonization have been responsible for this. During the great European assault on Africa, which reached its zenith during the last decades of the nineteenth century, the annexation of territory by the imperial powers took no account of the culture, history and social structures of the peoples who were conquered. The imperial powers invested in their African territories to extract profits, mostly through the export to Europe of minerals and agricultural staples. In South Africa, the quest was for diamonds and gold. Elsewhere it was for cocoa or copper.

Investments to construct railways, harbors and other infrastructure were aimed at facilitating the commerce between the imperial power and the colonial territory, with no regard for the economic development of the African territory's own internal commerce. These colonies were not countries in the making. The miserable conditions in which their populations labored did not place them on the road to greater human and material development, rather the reverse.

During the late 1950s to the early 1970s, the British, French, Belgians and Portuguese ended their formal sovereignty over their African territories. While the French gave up their hold on Algeria as a consequence of the bitter war for Algerian independence, most of the other imperial departures (Kenya was an exception) were not compelled by powerful insurgencies. In the space of a few years, members of the British royal family presided over ceremonies at which the Union Jack was lowered in a long list of countries, including Ghana, Nigeria, Kenya, Uganda, Tanzania and later Rhodesia (which became

Zimbabwe), following a period of minority white rule outside the framework of British control.

On the surface these appeared to be new countries, with their own capital cities, flags and boundaries, whose legacy from colonial rule were British-style parliaments, judicial systems and military uniforms. Terrible living conditions, indissolubly linked to continuing economic ties to former colonial powers (which had become neocolonial powers), and the emergence of underlying tribal, linguistic, religious and other realities soon combined to topple the weak institutional pillars on which these supposed democracies had been erected.

Multiparty democratic governments soon crumbled as strongmen seized power, often relying on their ties to the military to carry out coups. In Uganda, for instance, in January 1971, Idi Amin used his position as head of the country's fledgling army to seize power, dispense with democratic institutions and commence a reign of terror that resulted in the deaths of tens of thousands of people. The year after taking power, Amin launched a campaign against Uganda's large Asian (mostly Indian) population, whose members made up an important part of the country's commercial class. As a consequence of this vendetta against them, 80,000 Asians were expelled from Uganda, fleeing to Britain, Canada and Sweden among other places.

Following the establishment of states that were formally sovereign, sub-Saharan Africa continued to be a chessboard where the great powers played out their rivalries in their struggles to gain advantage in the quest for raw materials and geo-political leverage. During the Cold War, the United States and the Soviet Union backed their favorite political leaders and political factions, as did Britain and France, and schemed to undermine those who threatened their interests. Since the demise of the Soviet Union, China has become a key player in many countries in Africa, including war-torn Sudan, the setting for ethnic cleansing on a massive scale.

Between 1956 and 1985, there were sixty successful coups d'état in Africa, involving the violent replacement of one regime by another. In a large number of these struggles, the great powers were involved. For instance, in 1961, Patrice Lumumba, the popular elected leader of the Congo, was removed from office and assassinated in a violent coup in which American and Belgian interests were involved. In Ghana, the widely respected leader Kwame Nkrumah, who aimed to lessen the influence of outside powers in Africa, was expelled from office in a CIA-backed coup.

Rwanda, a former German and later Belgian colony, exploded in the 1990s. Half a million Tutsis were murdered by Hutus, in part as a consequence of the differing treatment of these two tribes by their rulers during colonial times. The country's severe shortage of arable land was also an important factor in triggering the genocide.

The Rwandan genocide was an extreme case, but there were numerous wars, secessionist movements and violent suppressions of tribal and religious minorities. In a number of cases, young boys were kidnapped and dragooned into the role of child soldiers. Systematic rape was an all-too-common accompaniment to these struggles. Warfare and civil strife exacerbated the continent's AIDS epidemic, worsened the effects of droughts and food shortages, and drove people out of their homes and into refugee camps.

The African tragedy is a product of world history over the past five centuries, and solutions need to come from movements for democracy, human rights and economic development in sub-Saharan Africa in conjunction with initiatives from the outside that are no longer driven by the motives that underlay colonialism and neo-colonialism. In Africa, genuine democracy must involve much more than the formal trappings of multiparty elections, important as those are. Genuine democracy cannot be achieved apart from struggles to end the role of outside great powers as sponsors of political factions and as the dominant forces behind violent changes of government and civil wars.

Chapter 6
Plutocracy, Globalization and Free Trade

In recent decades, as the US has emerged as the only superpower in the world, and as the gap between the wealthy and the rest of the American population has yawned ever wider, American democracy has faced mounting threats to its efficacy. In his farewell address, President Dwight D. Eisenhower warned of the dangers of the "military-industrial" complex to the future well-being of the United States. Since that address in 1961, corporate power, often tied to the military, has grown enormously, and its influence on government dangerously interferes with that of the citizenry. In the US, democracy is under threat from plutocracy, a political system in which huge sums of money are necessary for the achievement of high office, both at the federal level and at the state level.

Democracy and Plutocracy in the US
Thomas Jefferson believed that the commitment of the American Republic to the principles on which it was founded depended on the yeoman class. By this he meant

the farmers of small independent farms who owned their property and worked their land. Over the long term, of course, the US ceased to be a predominantly agrarian country. In the decades that followed the Civil War (1861–1865), a new US was shaped by the tycoons who dominated whole sectors of the economy – John D. Rockefeller at Standard Oil, Andrew Carnegie at US Steel, Henry Ford at the Ford Motor Company and John Pierpont Morgan Jr. (son of the industrialist and financier J.P. Morgan), the great banker and financial capitalist. These figures overshadowed political leaders and they bought politicians when they needed their favors. When they had to, they hired goons to break up trade unions that threatened to organize their employees. President Calvin Coolidge summed up their values in the 1920s when he proclaimed that "the business of America is business."

The battle between "big money" and American democracy became a permanent feature of American life. Sometimes the big interests were winning and sometimes the great reformers who infused new strength into American democracy carried the day.

Following the First World War, big business swept all before it, and the forces of reform were weakened by the Red Scare and the notorious Palmer raids (named for Woodrow Wilson's Attorney General Alexander Mitchell Palmer, who presided over them) in which trade union-ists and political radicals were rounded up and jailed, and even framed for crimes they did not commit. The targets of the crackdown were often charged with sedition under the Sedition Act of 1918, which sought to criminalize the advocacy of radical change.

In 1933, though, the greatest reforming president of the twentieth century, Franklin Delano Roosevelt, came to office during the worst days of the Great Depression. Roosevelt, himself the heir to great wealth, was a champion of working people and the unemployed, and was often viewed as a traitor to his own social class. Roosevelt's New Deal grew out of and contributed to the development of a broad new democratic alliance that included working people, trade unionists, farmers, recent immigrants, intellectuals, writers and filmmakers, as well as most of the African Americans who had the vote at the time (those outside the South).[1]

This was the political alliance that established social security (income for retirement), the nation's most essential social program. The same coalition oversaw America's role in the Second World War and the transition to peace after 1945. Despite the politics of fear fostered by McCarthyism in the 1950s (named for Senator Joseph McCarthy of Wisconsin, who held congressional hearings exposing persons alleged to be Communists or Communist sympathizers), the political and social coalition that had established the New Deal and won the war held together to bring John F. Kennedy to the presidency by the narrowest of margins in the 1960 election.

The greatest achievements during this final chapter in the history of Franklin Delano Roosevelt's coalition came following the assassination of John F. Kennedy in 1963. Under President Lyndon Johnson, the US Congress passed the reforms that assured the vote to African Americans, outlawed what remained of racial segregation and launched the War on Poverty. These reforms provoked an enormous political backlash among white Southerners, who switched their political allegiance en masse from the Democrats to the Republicans. The great postwar age of American industrialism, the high point of trade unionism in the US, came to an end as a consequence of a rising tide of imports from Japan, West Germany and the beginning of what was to become a flood of imports from low-wage developing countries.

As the markets and production facilities of US-based multinational corporations spread all over the world, wages and salaries in the US and other advanced countries stopped rising. In sharp contrast to the period from 1950 to 1970 in the US and Canada when the real incomes of wage and salary earners (accounting for inflation) doubled, between 1980 and the present there has been no rise in the real incomes of typical wage and salary earners. By 2007, the share of the national income accounted for by wages and salaries in the US was the same as it had been in 1928. All the gains working people had made in the proportion of the national income they enjoyed during the postwar decades had disappeared. Top executives of major corporations who had made forty times as much as one of their average employees in 1980 were making more than a hundred times as much and sometimes two hundred times as much as those who worked for them.

Along with the soaring power of business in relation

to labor came a corresponding increase in the role of money in politics. By the 1990s, American democracy was morphing into plutocracy, a system in which the power of wealth and money play an ever-increasing role in determining political outcomes.

In 1992, the American economy was recovering from a severe recession, a recession whose force had sapped the strength of President George Bush. The year 1992 is best remembered for the emergence of Bill Clinton who defeated George Bush with the slogan, "It's the economy, stupid!" When historians in the future look back on that presidential election, they may focus as much on the man who ran third in the race, Ross Perot. Perot's quixotic campaign in 1992 transformed American politics.

What made Perot a unique figure is that he concluded that he should take a run for the presidency, not as the culmination of a life of political activity in one of the nation's two major political parties, but following a career in business that had earned him great personal wealth. What made people take him seriously was the vast amount of his own money that he was prepared to lavish on his campaign. Perot did have a folksy way of communicating with ordinary people, and he managed to connect by saying that his experience in business made him well-suited to running the business of America. But it was his money that spoke loudest.

Rich men had run for president before as the candidates of the Democratic and Republican parties. Two wealthy Roosevelts — Theodore, a Republican, and Franklin, a Democrat — won the nation's highest office.

Never before, however, had a candidate running as an independent, with money alone as his qualification, made a serious run for the presidency.

Since Perot's pioneering entry into American politics at the highest level, in presidential campaigns in 1992 and 1996, others have followed in his footsteps. Steve Forbes, the wealthy publisher, took a run at the Republican presidential nomination in 1996 and 2000. Although he was particularly lacking in the performing talents that are necessary to a successful politician, he managed to wage a national campaign on the basis of his affluence alone.

Far more important than Forbes, however, was George W. Bush. Bush's campaign in 2000 not only brought to office a candidate who had not won the most votes for the first time in many decades, it brought to office a candidate whose campaign was far more flush with money than any previous one.

Four years later, both Bush and his Democratic challenger, John Kerry, exceeded federal spending limits so that they did not receive matching funds from the federal government during their campaigns for their parties' nominations. As candidates in both parties made a run for their parties' presidential nominations in 2008, money played an even greater role. The price tag on the fight for the nomination and then for the general election dwarfed all the campaigns of the past. While the Republican Party nominee, Senator John McCain, did not have a huge war chest, the two leading candidates for the Democratic Party nomination, Senators Barack

Obama and Hillary Clinton, raised enormous sums and dispensed with federal funding during their long duel for their party's nomination. In June 2008, the Obama campaign announced that their candidate would forgo the matching federal government election funds, amounting to $84.1 million, and would rely on the funds it could raise on its own. This meant that there would be no spending limit on Obama's bid for the White House. It was the first time since the funding system went into effect in 1976 that a candidate representing a major party had not taken funds from the federal government for the period of the formal campaign in the autumn of the election year.

The trend toward plutocracy has been more pronounced in the US than elsewhere, but similar trends are evident in many other advanced countries, where democracy is at best holding its own, and may well be in decline.

Globalization and Free Trade

The principal driving force behind the rise of plutocracy has been globalization, and in particular, the impact of economic blocs such as the World Trade Organization, the European Union and the North American Free Trade Agreement. The World Trade Organization regulations surrounding the free flow of capital in the world place enormous restrictions on the power of national governments to restrain or shape the operations of the market to achieve social goals.

In Europe, the European Union has had a distinct

impact on the practice and perception of democracy. The EU now has twenty-seven member countries, with a total population of over 400 million people. The capacity of the EU to legislate on behalf of Europeans has increased dramatically since the process of union began in 1951, when six countries founded the European Coal and Steel Community (ECSC). Over the decades, the ECSC was followed by the European Economic Community, the Single Market, the Treaty of Maastricht (creating the European Union and European citizenship), the single currency (euro) for most EU member states, and the so-far unsuccessful effort to negotiate a treaty establishing an even closer political union.

The European Union is the world's leading case where democratic states have voluntarily pooled their sovereignty to establish a political and social, as well as economic, union. Every four years Europeans elect a European Parliament, which sits in Strasbourg, France, to pass legislation that is binding on all Europeans. In the European Parliament, parliamentarians address the issues in the many EU languages, with their speeches simultaneously translated into all the other languages. Delegations do not sit in national groupings but in political groupings that bring together those who share common outlooks. For instance, social democrats and socialists sit together in a European socialist grouping that includes, among others, German Social Democrats, French Socialists and British Labourites. The center right, including many Christian Democratic parties, sits together as the European People's Party.

These steps toward a common European polity constitute a staggering achievement. From a past in which the continent was torn by the deaths of millions in two world wars, Europe has established a common citizenship, freedom of mobility and a democratic structure for the EU that brings together peoples formerly bitterly divided by war and the threat of war.[2]

Yet popular politics in the EU today remains decidedly national in character in each member country. The political struggles in each country arise out of traditions that go back centuries. In France, for example, it is no exaggeration to say that political streams can trace their origins back to the French Revolution. The phases of the great revolution and the counter-revolution continue to have meaning in France in contemporary struggles for power. In Britain, as well, there are the unique political traditions of a country that has repelled all attempts of foreign invasion going back nine hundred years, and that are rooted in a very particular set of parliamentary institutions and a constitutional monarchy. The same can be said for each of the EU member states.

From the point of view of most Europeans, the European Union, despite its many advantages and achievements, is a highly bureaucratic, opaque and bafflingly complex set of institutions. EU decisions often appear to European citizens as arbitrary and meddlesome. Every European country is now replete with jokes about the impenetrable bureaucracy inhabited by the Eurocrats in Brussels. In fact, the EU bureaucracy is tiny in comparison to the bureaucracies of the member states, and all of the Eurocrats could be housed in a small corner of official Paris or London.

From Brussels come a series of edicts that have a very real impact on economic life in the member states. When a member state bestows a state subsidy or tax benefit on a homegrown industry, Brussels often rules that such measures violate European competition policies and must be removed. When such subsidies are in place to prevent local jobs from being lost, such EU decisions appear to thwart the right of democratically elected national governments to act on behalf of their own citizens. Brussels, in the eyes of many politicians in Europe, poses a constant threat to democracy.

The rapid expansion of the EU to a membership of twenty-seven nations has made its decision-making process both more unwieldy and less transparent than in the past. The EU is no longer a club of Western European countries with advanced economies and comparatively similar socio-economic systems. It now takes in Scandinavia, the countries of the Iberian Peninsula and the nations of Eastern Europe that were a part of the Soviet Empire prior to 1989. The cultural differences and the range of economic conditions and social arrangements are dauntingly vast.

To make the EU more effective as well as more democratic, efforts have been devoted to negotiate a new treaty that would give it even more authority. This, however, has generated a backlash among the citizens of many countries, people who are already alienated by the decline in national authority and are opposed to further centralization.

From a democratic standpoint, the EU is precariously perched between two stools — those of national and European authority. A major cultural and political shift would have to occur to make EU institutions genuinely democratic. No less than a European political culture would be needed for this. Except to a limited extent at the elite level, such a political culture shows little sign of emerging. When it comes to stirring themselves to participate in politics, the Poles, French, Germans and Italians remain decisively attached to their national political institutions and traditions. For the EU to function smoothly more power is needed at its center. It is difficult, however, to envisage how this can be achieved without an effective reduction in democracy at the level of ordinary citizens.

An issue that touches on the character of democracy in Europe concerns Turkey, which for many years has sought full membership in the European Union. A Muslim country located with one foot in Europe and one in Asia, Turkey is a member of the North Atlantic Treaty Organization (NATO). It is formally a democracy, but the military plays a key role in the Turkish state, and Turkish politics has been roiled in recent years by the rising influence of Islamist movements. In EU countries, public anxiety about admitting an Islamic country to the EU and the concern that Turkey is not a full-fledged democracy have so far kept the country with associate membership only.

The establishment of the Canada-US Free Trade Agreement (FTA) in 1989, and later the North American

Free Trade Agreement (NAFTA), including Mexico, in 1994 has had a significant effect on the character of Canadian democracy. Although the FTA and NAFTA were styled as agreements to create a free trade area, they included clauses that dramatically affected the flow of investment, rules on foreign ownership and the management of strategic resources.

For Canada and Mexico, and to a much lesser extent for the US as the dominant partner, NAFTA severely limited the powers of federal and provincial or state governments. Under the agreement, the member countries were required to accord "national treatment" to each other's companies. For Canadians, who had debated and passed legislation to control the vast extent of direct foreign investment (predominantly American) in Canada, the trade agreement limited the government's power to discriminate in favor of Canadian-owned firms through tax policies and subsidies.[3]

An undertaking of NAFTA that is little understood by the public in all three member countries is the treaty's Chapter 11. This chapter sharply restricts the right of member states to halt the shipment of particular commodities into their territory once trade in these commodities has commenced. For instance, once chemical companies begin the shipment of particular pesticides from the US to Canada, it is very difficult for the Canadian federal government or provincial governments to put a stop to these shipments on the grounds that a specific pesticide is environmentally dangerous or is hazardous to people's health. Attempts by governments to put new restrictions in place once trading in a commodity has begun opens the door for corporations to challenge the new regulations under the terms of Chapter 11. The onus is on the governments to justify their behavior rather than on the companies.

NAFTA also restricted the Canadian government's ability to manage Canada's petroleum industry. Under the agreement, Canada is barred from establishing a lower price for the domestic sale of its petroleum than for the sale of petroleum to the US. Moreover, Canada is committed to exporting petroleum to the US at the average level of the preceding three years. This commitment remains in place even in the event of shortages in regions of eastern Canada that are dependent on imports of foreign oil. An additional feature of the NAFTA treaty dramatically affects Canada. Under NAFTA, the US can countervail against Canadian imports (levy tariffs against them) should the Americans find the competition too stiff in a particular sector. The US has done exactly this for many years to limit Canadian exports of softwood lumber. In theory, Canada and Mexico can use their own trade laws to retaliate against such US use of its trade law. In practice, however, since these countries are so much more dependent on exports to the US than the US is on exports to them, this is too costly an option to deploy.

For Canada, NAFTA has proven to be a veritable fourth level of government, sitting atop the municipal, provincial and federal levels. Inaccessible to political decision-makers, it is also inaccessible to voters. It reduces the transparency and effectiveness of democratic

Voter Turnout		
Country	Voter Turnout 1960s	Voter Turnout 2000s
Canada	75.7% (1968)	59.1% (2008)
Denmark	89.3% (1968)	86.6% (2007)
France (Presidential)	84.2% (1965)	84% (2007)
France (National Assembly)	81.1% (1967)	60.4% (2007)
Germany	86.7% (1969)	77.7% (2005)
Iceland	91.4% (1967)	83.6% (2007)
India	60.9% (1967)	57.7% (2004)
Italy	92.8% (1968)	80.4% (2008)
Japan	74% (1967)	67.5% (2005)
Norway	83.8% (1969)	77.4% (2005)
United Kingdom	76% (1966)	61.4% (2005)
United States*	60.8% (1960)	60.7% (2008)

* Voters must choose to register in the US.

decision-making. From the point of view of the average citizen, the efficacy (the term political scientists use to mean the value) of participating in the political process is seriously diminished.

Globalization and the impact of free trade blocs have the effect of reinforcing the idea among typical citizens that there is little they can do to influence the political process. An important sign that for voters political efficacy is in decline is a decrease in the rate of voter turnout. This has decidedly been the case in Canada, where in federal elections participation has dropped over the past couple of decades from about 75 percent of the eligible electorate to only 59 percent.

Throughout the advanced world, mass political parties are waning in importance. In parliamentary systems such as those in Canada and the UK, presidential-style politics is on the rise. In Europe and North America, a struggle is underway between the forces of democracy and the forces that have established powerful economic blocs. How that struggle will be resolved will have large consequences for the vigor of democracy in the West.

Chapter 7
The Future of Democracy

As we have seen, democracy emerged in a particular historical and cultural setting as a consequence of specific social, political and economic struggles. There is no compelling evidence that there is a universal yearning for democracy in all cultures and social settings, and we can dispense with the dubious proposition that democracy is an outgrowth of human nature.

The appetite for democracy arises not from political theory but from the tangible needs of millions of people. Above all, democracy is advanced by the success of political movements whose goal is to improve the lives of the majority of the population in a number of ways. Democracy establishes the rights of people and the rules under which they behave toward one another in society. Included among these rights are free speech and freedom of assembly, rights that are fundamental for the advocacy of the political programs people wish to advance.

Shorn of rhetoric and boiled down to essentials, political programs proceed on two related but distinct levels. At the most general level, and with a long time horizon, there is the advocacy of how the state should be designed and whose interests it should serve. The state is not an abstraction — it is an enormous complex of institutions that have been established over a long period of time to achieve a wide range of goals.

States — all states for thousands of years — have claimed for themselves a monopoly on the means of violence (an ideal never achieved but much more closely approximated in some cases than in others). States act to protect the existing property arrangements in society, enforcing them through the deployment of police and other security forces, courts and penal institutions. Most states, for most of human history, have resorted to the widespread use of capital punishment. If security of property, the physical security of the population and the security of the regime in power were the overriding priorities of all states for most of human history, to these priorities have been added new objectives over the past two centuries.

In the latter half of the nineteenth century, in much of North America and Europe, governments became responsible for providing tuition-free schooling for all children at the primary level and later at the secondary level. This benefited both those receiving the education and employers, who needed an educated workforce. And following the Second World War, these governments became responsible for the pursuit of a much wider range of goals. As never before, they became charged with ensuring full employment, decent working conditions and with limiting the hours of work an employer could demand from employees. Governments took on the task in many jurisdictions of establishing a minimum wage through legislation. State expenditures skyrocketed for the provision of unemployment insurance, health care, welfare payments for those unable to work, pensions for senior citizens and payment for all or much of the cost of higher education.

Alongside these expenditures, modern states invest enormous sums in infrastructure that is invaluable to the private sector and critical to the effort to increase competitiveness against producers in other countries. States also invest heavily in supporting business through tax cuts, direct subsidies and the provision of services that help businesses to export or to acquire skilled labor.

On the more immediate level, political struggles in democratic countries are largely about which functions of the state should be enhanced and which should be reduced or curtailed.

Political parties on the right advocate tax cuts, especially for high-income earners who are also investors. They favor cutting the social expenditures of the state. They oppose increases in the minimum wage and more stringent maximum hours legislation. For instance, the French right was strongly opposed to the Socialist government's implementation of a thirty-five-hour work week in 2000. Parties on the right tend to oppose tougher environmental measures, which increase the costs of business. Right-wing parties advocate reducing legislated job security standards, making the case that this allows for a more "flexible" economy. They support, for example, reducing the length of time companies must make severance payments to terminated employees.

Left-wing parties take opposing positions on most of these issues. They favor increased state expenditures on social programs (such as welfare payments and child care) and education, and they advocate higher minimum wages and legislation that reduces the length of the work week. Left-wing parties support stronger environmental legislation and usually oppose tax cuts for business and high-income earners. The right and the left can sometimes find common ground on state expenditures for infrastructure programs.

These debates between the right and the left are debates about the nature of the state and which activities of the state should be enlarged or contracted. It boils down to whose interests the state should serve. More often than not, the fault line along which these debates run is that of social class. Parties of the right promote the interests of the private sector and investors, while left-wing parties champion the interests of wage and salary earners.

Voters often don't perceive the issues in these terms and vote for parties whose programs seem to contradict their class interests. Moreover, political leaders clothe their programs and long-term view of the state in language that embodies the traditions of their country and the rhetoric of past political conflicts.

While philosophers and political theorists debate the nature of democracy, political parties struggle on behalf of those whose interests they represent. This is the essen-

Voting Against Your Own Interests

A matter of recurring speculation among political analysts for more than a century is explaining why so many people apparently choose to "vote against their own interests." To put it more sharply, why do so many wage and salary earners, in addition to many who are trapped in poverty, vote for political parties whose programs quite explicitly favor the rich?

In the mid-nineteenth century, it was fashionable for politicians and writers who were concerned about the prospects of the well-to-do to fear that universal manhood suffrage (votes for all men) would inexorably lead to the election of governments that would favor the expropriation of the wealth of the few on behalf of the impoverished many. It has not turned out that way, however. While social democratic and socialist parties have regularly won office in a number of countries, very few democratically elected governments have set out to achieve a massive redistribution of wealth from the rich to the rest of the population. Why have votes for all men and eventually for all women posed such minor threats to the fundamental interests of the wealthy and of large corporations?

A host of factors account for why so many working-class voters support conservative political parties. They include the ethnic, racial, religious, national and regional antagonisms that have divided and continue to divide working-class people. In addition, there are the resentments of those with jobs against the unemployed and those on social assistance, and the envy of those who work in the private sector toward those in the public sector who enjoy greater job security. There is the feeling of many who do not enjoy the benefits of union membership that those who do have an unfair advantage. Not least, there is the awesome authority of those who hold power in the established order to convince a large proportion of the population that their modest share in the existing system is preferable to anything they might hope for in the struggle for a more equitable society.

tial battleground of democracy. At the heart of the democratic project, there is a premise that is always subject to doubt — that all persons, in a fundamental sense, are of equal value. Should the notion of equality perish, so too would the idea of democracy. And since the human condition in our time is one in which there are enormous differences of wealth, income and circumstance, the ideal of equality is endangered.

History and contemporary realities teach that the wealthy and privileged in any society have little basic attachment to the idea of equality. Once those who are the members of an upper class have secured their place in the world, they have shown themselves to be all too ready to pull up the ladder to prevent those below them from climbing to their level. For the most part, they would be content to hold onto a world in which their advantages are retained for themselves and passed on to their descendants.

It is therefore reasonable to posit that the flame of equality and consequently of democracy must be kept burning by the vast majority of the population that does not belong to the upper classes. The drive for equality and democracy mostly comes from below, not from above.

What are the prospects, in light of this, for equality and democracy in a globalized world reliant on advanced technology in which a few states have vastly more power (military, economic, political and cultural) than all the others combined?

The future of democracy will depend on social struggles as much in the future as its rise did in the past. Democracy is never standing still, a monument to past glories and ringing declarations. It is either advancing or retreating, and the advocates of democracy can never cease to press their case or their cause.

Paradoxically, the barriers in the way of democracy and the opportunities for its advance arise out of contradictory aspects of the same issues. Some of those issues, the great questions in our age that will determine the strength of democracy, are the wealth and income gaps, not only within particular countries, but between the advanced countries and the rest of the world; the availability of quality education for the whole population; universal health care; employment opportunities and job security; the struggle against the marginalization of people on the basis of ethnicity, race, gender, sexual orientation and religion; the containment of war and the prevention of the spread of ever more lethal weaponry; the opening of frontiers to allow people to migrate to the places where economic development compels them to go; and the safeguarding of the environment, including a halt to the wanton destruction of other species.

Each and all of these issues challenge the capacity of democrats, not only to draw on the best in their own national traditions, but to find ways to establish democratic cultures than can transcend frontiers. By the same token, these issues place immense barriers in the path of democracy for the simple reason that they can and will call forth agendas to preserve the advantages of privileged people, nations and cultures through the exclusion and marginalization of large parts of the population, and on some of the issues, the majority of the human race.

History shows that exceptionally powerful authoritarian political movements are capable of mobilizing millions of people to action to grapple with basic issues through programs that are the very antithesis of democracy. In the 1930s, the fascists and the Nazis demonstrated that when democrats dither and fail to come to grips with urgent problems, such as mass unemployment and poverty, others will not dither. And the solutions of the authoritarians can involve not merely the elimination of democratic rights but the imprisonment of thousands, and in the most extreme cases the murder of millions.

The vigor of democracy will depend on how democratic political parties and movements rise to the challenge, not only of the socio-economic and environmental problems that plague our world, but also to the campaigns of the intolerant who will use these problems to promote false solutions based on hate and scapegoating. Everywhere democrats look today, they observe the walls of hate going up in the form of anti-immigrant sentiment and religious fundamentalism.

For the past quarter century, democratic parties of all shades in Europe and North America have utterly failed to cope with the widening gap in income and wealth between a small segment of the population that has been enormously enriched and the vast majority of the population of the advanced countries, and much more so, the population of humanity as a whole. From center-right parties such as the German Christian Democrats to the

American Democrats and the French Socialists, solutions have not been found to halt the trajectory of a market-driven global economy toward increasingly pronounced inequality.

The issue of inequality and much more came to a head in September and October 2008, with the onset of the most serious global financial crisis since the Great Depression, which began in 1929. Financial institutions imploded, stock markets crashed, credit markets ceased to function, and governments were forced to bail out banks and other financial institutions at a cost of hundreds of billions of dollars. In some cases, notably that of the United Kingdom, the government nationalized banks. The market system, as the world has known it for the past three decades, collapsed in chaos. Governments stepped in hoping that their vast and concerted interventions would re-launch the economy. Resentment and fear stalked the nations of the world, as tens of millions of people concluded that they had been betrayed by their economic and political leaders.

The boiling anger of those who are shut off from the possibility of advance can open the door to a strengthened democracy, but it can also feed into the agenda of those who fabricate lies that the world is run by some ethnic or religious group that can be isolated and attacked. For the Nazis, the theory was that the world was run by Jewish financiers who had stabbed Germany in the back during the First World War.

Today, the world is alive with new theories that are used to marginalize people: in Europe, there is fear of

Muslim immigrants and their descendants; in the US, fear of Hispanic immigrants; and in many parts of the world there is propaganda from religious fundamentalists who seek to blame our ills on people of other faiths. These forms of hatred can be used to tell people that immigrants are taking jobs away from the French, that newcomers are robbing the American middle class of its standard of living, or that God has a divine plan for people of particular faiths that must not be thwarted by the designs of others.

While democracy faces stubborn barriers and is actually in decline in many parts of the world, movements have taken shape in recent years that are advancing the cause of democracy. The threats to democracy should not be underestimated, but neither should the forces that defend and extend it be discounted. From a wide range of sources — progressives, social democrats, socialists, humanists, environmentalists, non-fundamentalist religious believers, feminists, trade unionists, urban activists, anti-poverty activists, students and writers — a new politics of the planet has been taking shape. It is, of necessity, diverse, pluralist and democratic. Its philosophical origins are ancient as well as contemporary. This politics of the planet takes unique forms in each country, arising out of particular cultures and conditions.

The broad challenge to democrats is to reinvigorate democracy at the local and national levels, while advancing programs that for the first time in history are in keeping with the interests of people everywhere. The perspective has to be planetary. But unlike the corporate agenda

Democracies Fall Short of the Ideal

The ancient Greeks distinguished democracy from autocracy, rule by a single leader; monarchy, rule by a hereditary king; aristocracy, rule by a privileged nobility; oligarchy, rule by a few; and plutocracy, rule by the wealthy. Few societies or states come close to being perfect embodiments of any one of these systems of government.

In the early years of the twenty-first century, money has become an ever more important ingredient in politics. The 2008 American presidential election was a $1 billion affair, by far the most expensive in American history. The growing power of money in American politics indicates that along with democracy, America is governed by plutocracy as well as by a political class that displays more than a few of the features of an oligarchy.

Other states have displayed the features of various other forms of governance. For instance, Nazi Germany (1933 to 1945) was one of the most extreme cases of autocracy in the history of the world. Even Nazi Germany, however, was not a pure case of autocracy. Along with Adolf Hitler, the leader, an extremely powerful oligarchy of subordinate governors competed fiercely with one another for additional power in running elements of the military, industry and the state, and they vied for the favor of the supreme leader.

In Britain, along with democracy, elements of aristocracy and oligarchy as well as plutocracy have been important features of the system of governance. British voters had to share power with the hereditary House of Lords well into the twentieth century. While its power was curtailed by an Act of Parliament in 1911 and has been further reduced by subsequent reforms, the aristocracy has clung to considerable political and societal authority. This authority is sustained, in part, through the important role played in Britain by private schools (known as independent or public schools) to which the affluent send their children, along with elite universities, Oxford and Cambridge. Many top British politicians, including many prime ministers have attended these schools. In the early twenty-first century, Britain has a democratic political system with important overlays of aristocratic influence as well as the strong influence of a rather narrow and oligarchic political class.

that has stripped away power from the level of the nation-state, the democratic agenda needs to return effective power to nations so they can design their social systems, govern their own economies and act as stewards for their share of the planet.

If this sort of agenda sounds as though it is alive with paradox and contradiction, it is. It is the reverse of much that has driven the global agenda of the past three decades during the so-called age of globalization. Globalization has, in truth, drawn all people and all nations into a closer set of relationships with one another. But the relationships have been based on amplifying the power of the few at the expense of the many on a wide range of fronts, so much so that we can conclude that globalization has effectively paralyzed democracy to an alarming extent.

While it has been claimed by its proponents that globalization has opened borders and reduced the power of the state, in fact, globalization has opened borders to the flow of capital and has reduced the power of most of the states of the world, leaving the socio-economic future to be shaped by a handful of states (the United States most important among them), while borders have been closed to most of humanity.

A case in point is the plight of desperate people who take to flimsy vessels to sail from Africa to Europe in the hope that they will be able to make a living there for themselves and their families. All too often they die during the voyage. Similarly, tens of thousands of Mexicans take their lives into their hands each year, attempting to make it past the growing army of border guards into the US. There they can work for low pay and with no job protection in a country where the political rhetoric has increasingly reduced them to the status of pariahs. The American economy would be hard pressed to function without these illegal immigrants, but on the political right politicians advocate the denial of all social and educational benefits to these workers and their children. Across the developed world, the barriers are going up to stop desperate economic refugees from reaching the promised land.

At the same time, as the wretched and poor are deprived of access to countries where they can make a living, the wealthy have turned the whole world, or at least those parts of it that are not too dangerous to visit, into their playground. They leave their ultra-expensive dwellings in the heart of London, for instance, in the care of the Polish or Czech au pairs and servants in their employ, and take their children during half-term breaks from their private schools and fly off to South Africa, India, Bali or Bahrain for their holidays in luxurious surroundings. They can travel, while the wretched over whose countries they fly are shut out of the wider world.

The democratic agenda needs to regard this staggering inequality as the most important matter to be addressed. Unless it is effectively addressed, little else that is achieved will matter very much.

Putting the world on the road toward equality will call forth as much creative energy as the great democratic upheavals of the eighteenth century. Power needs to be returned to nation-states so that their citizens can address inequality within their countries at the same time as an agenda to confront the inequality between nations is established. Such a power shift can only be achieved through the mobilization of the democratic energies of a wide spectrum of the population.

It's not hard to locate the issue on which this majority can be mobilized. Wage and salary earners in the developed world are on an economic treadmill. On average their living standards have not risen for the past several decades, and they are increasingly plunging into debt to finance the purchase of homes and to send their children to post-secondary educational institutions whose tuitions have been skyrocketing. The huge economic gains of this period have gone only to a few.

Wage and salary earners are increasingly conscious of the emergence of levels of inequality that have not been seen since the aristocratic age that preceded the American and French Revolutions. Those at the helm of the advanced economies tout the idea of "flexibility," the notion that the investment of capital and the location of enterprises should be directed by the marketplace to wherever in the world they can be most effective. One respected voice representing this point of view is the *Economist* weekly magazine in London. On January 20, 2007, it proclaimed that "these are the glory days of global capitalism...This newspaper has long argued that a mobile society is better than an equal one."

The argument being made in these pages, with which many with the point of view of the *Economist* will stoutly disagree, is that inequality has gone too far to be compatible with a vigorous democracy. Returning a good deal of economic sovereignty to nation-states does not mean erecting economic walls around countries. That is neither desirable nor possible in our age. What it means, above all, is a shift in the control of capital from the ever larger financial holdings that now exist to local, regional or national holdings.

What has this to do with the future of democracy? one may ask. It has as much to do with the future of democracy as the dividing up of the huge estates and the redistribution of land to the peasants in France in 1789 had to do with establishing a future for democracy at that time.

Over the longer term, a vibrant democracy is not compatible with the existence of ever larger pools of capital controlled privately. In such a world, the votes of people count for less and the votes of dollars and euros count for more. Placing pools of capital in local, regional and national holdings, and democratizing both the control of capital and of the workplace needs to be the next great chapter in the history of democracy. There is, to be sure, no easy fit between this step and the one that needs to accompany it — the establishment of a much more equitable relationship between the wealthy and the poor countries of the world.

Will advantageously placed nations use their privileged positions to assure more for themselves than for those with whom they conduct commerce in poorer countries? The short answer is yes, certainly. But in a world with capital pools divided up into local, regional and national holdings, the balance of power could effectively shift toward a new, democratic political coalition involving rich and poor countries. A politics of local, national and global development dedicated toward more egalitarian outcomes and sustainable environmental policies could emerge.

It is a hope, but a hope rooted in the realities of our world. Democracy has always been rooted in hope.

Democracy Timeline

Fifth century BC Male citizens of Athens over the age of eighteen assemble to pass legislation and make decisions for the Athenian state.

Fourth century BC Plebeians, the non-aristocratic citizens of Rome, acquire the right to participate in the election of consuls and other top officeholders.

1776 The Continental Congress adopts the Declaration of Independence, proclaiming the United States independent of Great Britain.

1783 Great Britain and the United States sign the Treaty of Paris, recognizing the United States as an independent country.

1787 At Philadelphia, the constitutional convention drafts the Constitution of the United States. When it came into effect, it replaced the first US Constitution, the Articles of Confederation, adopted in 1781.

1789 The French Revolution begins.

The French National Assembly abolishes the ownership of farmland by the aristocrats and passes the land to the serfs who farm it.

The French National Assembly adopts the Declaration of the Rights of Man and Citizen, recognized as a forerunner of the United Nations Universal Declaration of Human Rights.

1792 British writer and feminist Mary Wollstonecraft publishes *A Vindication of the Rights of Woman* in which she makes the case that women should be accorded full political rights.

1807 The Latin American wars of independence against Spanish
rule begin. They continue for several decades.

1863 During the Civil War, the US federal government issues the
Emancipation Proclamation, an edict that declares "that all
persons held as slaves" within the rebellious states "are,
and henceforward shall be free."

1865 The Thirteenth Amendment of the US Constitution proclaims that slavery is unconstitutional.

1870 The Fifteenth Amendment of the US Constitution proclaims
that American citizens cannot be denied the right to vote
on the basis of race.

1913 Norwegian women win the right to vote.

1919 Canadian women gain the right to vote in federal elections.

1920 The Nineteenth Amendment of the US Constitution establishes the right of women to vote.

1929 In London, the Judicial Committee of the Privy Council, the
highest court in the British Empire, rules that under the
terms of the British North America Act (Canada's constitution at the time) women are "persons," and therefore are
eligible to be appointed to the Senate.

1930 Mahatma Gandhi leads his historic salt march to Dandi to
mobilize the people of India against British rule.

1946 Japan's post-war democratic constitution is promulgated.

1948 The General Assembly of the United Nations, meeting in
Paris, adopts the Universal Declaration of Human Rights.

1949 The Federal Republic of Germany is established, creating a
system of proportional representation widely admired
around the world.

1951 Japan resumes full sovereignty when the country's peace treaty with the US and its allies goes into effect.

1989 The Berlin wall is opened. Over the next two years, Soviet-backed Communist regimes in Eastern Europe and the Soviet Union itself collapse, being replaced, in most cases, by democratic regimes.

1990 General Augusto Pinochet is forced to cede power in Chile, a key step in the resumption of democracy in that country.

African National Congress leader Nelson Mandela is released from prison. A few days before Mandela's release, South African president F.W. de Klerk ends the ban on the ANC.

1994 Nelson Mandela is inaugurated as South African president, following elections in which all adults – black, colored, Asian and white – participate.

2005 Evo Morales, a former coca farmer, becomes the first indigenous person to be elected president of Bolivia.

2008 Barack Obama becomes the first African American to be elected president of the United States.

Notes

1 What Is Democracy?
1. Jean Jacques Rousseau, *The Social Contract and Discourses* (Rockport, Illinois: BN Publishing, 2007).
2. All references to currency are in US dollars.

2 The Historical Rise of Democracy
1. Samuel Eliot Morison and Henry Steele Commager, *The Growth of the American Republic,* vol. 1 (New York: Oxford University Press, 1962), 189-91.
2. The phrase is from "Concord Hymn" (1837), a poem by Ralph Waldo Emerson that describes the battle:
"By the rude bridge that arched the flood,
Their flag to April's breeze unfurled,
Here once the embattled farmers stood
And fired the shot heard round the world."
3. Morison and Commager, *The Growth of the American Republic*, 274-94.
4. For a fine overview of the French Revolution see Georges Lefebvre, Timothy Tackett and R.R. Palmer, *The Coming of the French Revolution* (Princeton: Princeton Classic Editions, 2005) and Georges Lefebvre, *The French Revolution from 1793 to 1799* (New York: Columbia University Press, 1964).

3 Democratic Rights for Women and Racial and Religious Minorities
1. Eleanor Flexner, *Century of Struggle: The Woman's Rights Movement in the United States* (Boston: Harvard, 1959).
2. Henry David Thoreau, "Civil Disobedience," http://thoreau.eserver.org/civil.html
3. Ibid.
4. Ibid.
5. Robert J. Sharpe and Patricia I. McMahon, *The Persons Case: The*

Origins and Legacy of the Fight for Legal Personhood (Toronto: University of Toronto Press, 2007).

6. Melanie Phillips, *The Ascent of Woman: A History of the Suffragette Movement* (London: Little, Brown, 2003).

7. Greg Hurrell, "Henrik Ibsen, Frederika Bremer, Marie Michelet and the Emancipation of Women in Norway," Celsius Center for Scandinavian Studies, Vol. 2, 1998.

8. Allen C. Guelzo, *Lincoln's Emancipation Proclamation: The End of Slavery in America* (New York: Simon and Schuster, 2004).

9. James Laxer, *The Acadians: In Search of a Homeland* (Toronto: Doubleday Canada, 2006), pp. 168, 169.

10. Jane Dailey, Glenda Elizabeth Gilmore and Bryant Simon, eds. *Jumpin' Jim Crow: Southern Politics from Civil War to Civil Rights* (Princeton: Princeton University Press, 2000).

11. Richard Kluger, *Simple Justice: The History of Brown v. Board of Education and Black America's Struggle for Equality* (New York: Random House, 1975).

4 Democracy and the Demise of the Soviet Union

1. When I drove into Berlin, across East Germany, a month later, the demolition was still underway and there remained a great deal of wall to go around. I treasure the two pieces I acquired and keep on my desk.

2. See, for instance, Havel's 1989 collection of essays, *Living in Truth* (London: Faber and Faber, 1987).

3. I was in Wenceslas Square in the heart of Prague on July 3, 1990, the day Havel was sworn in as the country's president. I also traveled to Budapest during the election campaign and visited the headquarters of the contending parties. For a broader discussion of the revolutions in Eastern Europe, see James Laxer, *Inventing Europe: The Rise of a New World Power* (Toronto: Lester Publishing, 1991), Chapter 9.

4. As a consequence of the human rights violations and war crimes in the former Yugoslavia, the International Criminal Court (based in The Hague in the Netherlands) charged Serb military and politi-

cal leaders with genocide and crimes against humanity. The court succeeded in arresting and trying the former Serb president Slobodan Milosevic. Two years into his trial, and with no verdict having been rendered, Milosevic died in custody. In July 2008, after thirteen years in hiding, former Bosnian Serb leader Radovan Karadzic was arrested and is being tried by the ICC.

5. William C. Cockerham, "The Social Determinants of the Decline of Life Expectancy in Russia and Eastern Europe: A Lifestyle Explanation," *Journal of Health and Social Behavior*, Vol. 38, No. 2 (June 1997).

5 Movements for Democracy in the Developing World

1. Declassified US CIA Directorate of Intelligence research study, "Indonesia — 1965: The Coup That Backfired," 1968. (http://newsc.blogspot.com/).

2. Aung San Sui Kyi's acceptance message for the 1990 Sakharov Prize for Freedom of Thought (July 1991).

3. Gerald Caplan, *The Betrayal of Africa* (Toronto: Groundwood Books, 2008), 10.

6 Plutocracy, Globalization and Free Trade

1. On the changing nature of American politics, see Richard Hofstadter, *The American Political Tradition* (New York: A.A. Knopf, 1948).

2. For a history of the movement for European integration, see James Laxer, *Inventing Europe: The Rise of a New World Power* (Toronto: Lester Publishing, 1991).

3. Duncan Cameron and Mel Watkins, *Canada Under Free Trade* (Toronto: James Lorimer & Company, 1993).

For Further Information

Caplan, Gerald. *The Betrayal of Africa*. Toronto: Groundwood Books, 2008.

Dahl, Robert A. *On Democracy*. New Haven: Yale University Press, 1998.

King, Martin Luther, Jr. *Why We Can't Wait.* New York: Signet, 1964.

Livesey, James. *Making Democracy in the French Revolution*. Boston: Harvard University Press, 2001.

Lloyd, Trevor. *Suffragettes International: The World-wide Campaign for Women's Rights*. New York: American Heritage Press, 1971.

Macpherson, C.B. *The Life and Times of Liberal Democracy*. Oxford: Oxford University Press, 1977.

Mill, John Stuart. *On Liberty*. Filiquarian Publishing, 2006.

Moore, Barrington, Jr. *Social Origins of Dictatorship and Democracy*. Boston: Beacon Press, 1971.

Thoreau, Henry David. *Civil Disobedience and Other Essays*. New York: Dover Publications, 1993.

Tilly, Charles. *Contention and Democracy in Europe, 1650-2000*. Cambridge: Cambridge University Press, 2003.

Tocqueville, Alexis de. *Democracy in America*. New York: Everyman's Library, 1994.

Acknowledgments

It is a pleasure to be involved again in what is becoming such an influential series of books.

My thanks to Patsy Aldana for involving me in the series for the third time.

It has been a great pleasure to work once more with Jane Springer, who has made an invaluable contribution to conceiving the scope of this book and editing it. Thanks to Jackie Kaiser, my literary agent, for all her help.

Sandy, my partner, continues to share in my projects, and I have the pleasure of sharing in hers.

I am very grateful to everyone at Groundwood for support and for making such a success of the series. Michael Solomon, Nan Froman, Kelly Joseph, Fred Horler and Kate McQuaid have done a wonderful job. And thanks to Gillian Watts for the index.

Index

Holliston Public Library
Holliston, MA 01746

Many people assume that as societies become more advanced economically, they tend to become more democratic. It is also regularly assumed that democracy is on the rise in most parts of the world. Both assumptions are mistaken.

In *Democracy*, political scientist James Laxer shows that democracy arose as a consequence of very specific historical circumstances — and that there is no general tendency for it to progress. Not only is democracy a fugitive in most of the Middle East, China, much of the rest of Asia and in much of Africa, it faces increasing obstacles in North America and Europe.

Laxer's examination of the current status of democracy in the advanced countries, and in Asia, Africa, the Middle East and Latin America, clearly demonstrates that democracy is about much more than the right to vote. Globalization and the widening gap between the rich and the rest of the population everywhere around the world threaten to weaken democracy and the vigor of democratic regimes, even in countries where it has been long established. And in much of the West, especially in the US, Laxer shows that democracy is under threat from plutocracy — a political system in which huge sums of money are necessary for the achievement of high office.

THE GROUNDWORK GUIDES PROVIDE AN OVERVIEW OF KEY CONTEMPORARY POLITICAL AND SOCIAL ISSUES. ENGAGING, CONCISE AND CLEARLY WRITTEN, THESE BOOKS TACKLE PRESSING AND SOMETIMES CONTROVERSIAL TOPICS, OFFERING BOTH A LIVELY INTRODUCTION TO THE SUBJECT AND A STRONG POINT OF VIEW.

Award-winning author James Laxer has written twenty-one books, including the Groundwork Guides *Empire* and *Oil, The Acadians: In Search of a Homeland, Stalking the Elephant: My Discovery of America,* and *The Border: Canada, the U.S. and Dispatches from the 49th Parallel*. James Laxer appears regularly on television discussions of issues of the day. He was the h[...] global economy produced by the National Film [...] fessor of political science at York University in [...]

$11.00 CANADA / $10.00 US
Photograph © Pierre Holtz/epa/Corbis
Design by Lure Design Inc. (www. luredesigninc.com)
Distributed in the USA by Publishers Group West
Printed and bound in Canada

Groundwood Books / House of Anansi Press
www.groundwoodbooks.com

ISBN 978-0-88899-913-9